Excel 4 for Windows
The Visual Learning Guide

Watch for these forthcoming titles in this series:

Word for Windows 2: The Visual Learning Guide
1-2-3 for Windows: The Visual Learning Guide
WordPerfect for Windows: The Visual Learning Guide

Available Now!

Windows 3.1: The Visual Learning Guide
Excel 4 for Windows: The Visual Learning Guide

How to Order:

Quantity discounts are available from the publisher, Prima Publishing, P.O. Box 1260EXC, Rocklin, CA 95677; telephone (916) 786-0449. On your letterhead include information concerning the intended use of the books and the number of books you wish to purchase.

Excel 4 for Windows
The Visual Learning Guide

Grace Joely Beatty, Ph.D.

David C. Gardner, Ph.D.

Prima Publishing
P.O. Box 1260EXC
Rocklin, CA 95677
(916) 786-0426

Managing Editor: Roger Stewart
Project Manager: Laurie Stewart
Production: Marian Hartsough Associates
Interior Design: Grace Joely Beatty, S. Linda Beatty, David C. Gardner, Laurie Stewart, and Kim Bartusch
Technical Editing: Harriet Serenkin
Copyediting: Chet Bell
Cover Design: Kirschner-Caroff Design
Color Separations: Ocean Quigley
Index: Katherine Stimson

Prima Publishing
Rocklin, CA 95677-1260

Library of Congress Cataloging-in-Publication Data

Beatty, Grace Joely, 1947–
Excel 4 for Windows : the visual learning guide / Grace Joely Beatty and David C. Gardner
    p.   cm. — (Prima visual learning guides)
Includes index.
ISBN 1-55958-211-1 : $19.95
1. Microsoft Excel 4 for Windows.   2. Business—Computer programs.
3. Electronic spreadsheets.   4. Windows (Computer programs)
I. Title.   II. Title: Excel four for Windows.
HF5548.4.M523V354   1992
650' .0285 ' 5369—dc20
                   92-14150
                   CIP

92 93 94 95 RRD 10 9 8 7 6 5 4 3 2

Printed in the United States of America

Acknowledgments

Our lives have been enriched personally and professionally by so many people while writing this series.

Bill Gladstone of Waterside Productions, whose faith in us never wavered and who, with Matt Wagner, created the idea for this series.

We feel fortunate, indeed, in our association with Prima Publishing. We appreciate Ben Dominitz' personal involvement and support. Roger Stewart, our editor, is wonderful beyond words. Laurie Stewart, our project manager, is an author's dream. Her involvement helped create a book of which we are very proud. Debbie Parisi has done a wonderful job on PR, and Kim Bartusch helped create exciting graphics.

We have a terrific support team. Harriet Serenkin, our technical editor, is a joy to work with. Chet Bell edits our material almost overnight. Ocean Quigley, our color separator, has anguished through multiple conversions with us and has gone far beyond what duty requires.

Joseph and Shirley Beatty made this series possible. We can never repay them.

Paula Gardner Capaldo and David Capaldo have been terrific. Thanks, Joshua and Jessica, for being such wonderful kids! Special thanks to Stephen Capaldo.

Asher Shapiro has always been there when we needed him.

Carolyn Holder is our friend and beta tester extraordinaire. Her feedback made a big difference in the book! Thanks, Ray, for bringing her into our lives.

We worked with numerous reviewers around the country who gave generously of their time so that others could master Excel. David Coburn, Tom and Maura Healy, Matt Mancuso, Khoa Pham, David Sauer, and Michael Torre cannot be thanked enough!

We could not have kept the ball rolling without the following technical support: Fred Harper of Dymerc International and Michael Ayotte of Applications Techniques, Inc. We would also like to thank the technical support people at Excel. They were all unfailingly patient and informative.

Contents at a Glance

CONTENTS

Customize Your Learning

Prima *Visual Learning Guides* are not like any other computer books you have ever seen. They are based on our years in the classroom, our corporate consulting, and our research at Boston University on the best ways to teach technical information to non-technical learners. Most important, this series is based on the feedback of a panel of reviewers from across the country who range in computer knowledge from "panicked at the thought" to sophisticated.

This is not an everything-you've-ever-wanted-to-know-about-Excel 4-but-didn't-know-enough-to-ask book. It is designed to give you the information you need to perform basic (and some not-so-basic) functions with confidence and skill. It is a book that our reviewers claim makes it "really easy" for anyone to learn Excel 4 quickly.

Each chapter is illustrated with full-color screens to guide you through every task. The combination of screens, step-by-step instructions, and pointers makes it impossible for you to get lost or confused as you follow along on your own computer. You can either work through from the beginning to the end or skip around to master the skills you need. If you have a specific goal you want to accomplish now, choose it from the following list.

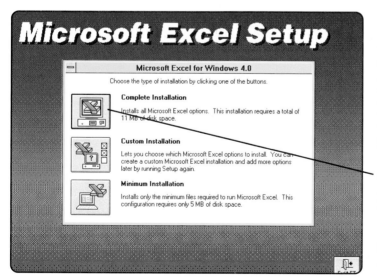

SELECT YOUR GOALS

From the list below, select your personal goals so you can start using Excel 4 immediately.

❖ I would like help installing Excel 4 for Windows.

Go to the appendix, "Installing Excel 4."

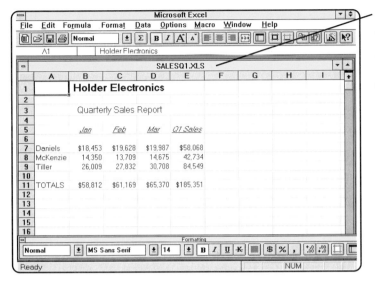

❖ I'm new to Excel and I want to learn how to set up a basic worksheet.

Turn to Part I, "Creating a Basic Worksheet," to create a basic worksheet. Then go to Part II, "Adding Style to Your Worksheet," to customize the worksheet.

To learn how to write formulas, turn to Chapter 13, "Writing Formulas."

❖ I would like to learn how to work with multiple worksheets.

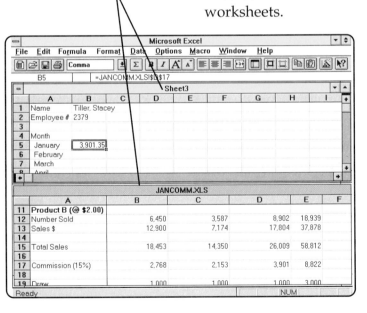

Turn to Part III, "Multiple Worksheets and Formulas." In this part, you will also learn how to link worksheets together so they share common information.

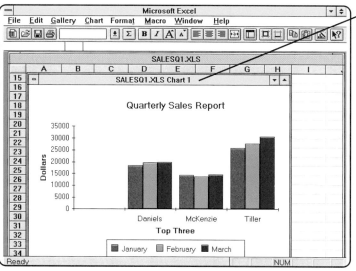

❖ I want to create and save a chart to illustrate the information on my worksheet.

Turn to Chapters 17, 18, 19, and 20 to create, print, and save a basic chart.

(If you have not developed a worksheet from which to make a chart, go to Part I first.)

If you want to add style to your chart by adding chart text, arrows, hatches, and shapes, go on to Chapters 21, 22, and 23.

❖ I want to paste a copy of a chart into a word processed document.

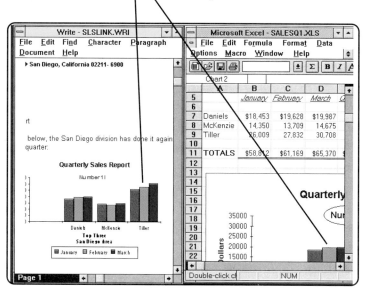

Go to Chapter 24, "Copying and Pasting a Chart."

❖ I would like to learn about the linking feature of Excel 4 for Windows.

Go to Chapter 25, "Copying and Linking a Chart."

Program Manager

Part I: Creating a Basic Worksheet

Setting Up a New Worksheet

The philosophy of the *Visual Learning Guide* series is that people learn best by doing. In this chapter you will:

❖ Create a basic worksheet

❖ Increase the width of a column to accommodate a long entry

❖ Sort a column alphabetically

❖ Learn how to use the on-line tutorial

If you haven't installed Excel yet, turn to the Appendix, "Installing Excel 4."

OPENING EXCEL FOR THE FIRST TIME

1. Type win at the C:\> (C prompt) on your screen to boot up Windows if it is not already on your screen. Since Windows provides for tremendous customization, you will probably have different group icons at the bottom of your screen than you see in this example.

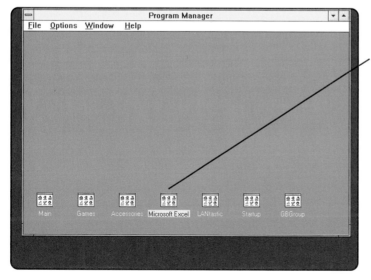

Depending on how Excel was installed on your computer, there may be a separate group icon for Microsoft Excel 4.0 at the bottom of your screen. Or Excel may have been moved to another group window. (See the Appendix for directions on how to move the Excel icon into a customized group window.)

In this example, Excel was moved to a customized group, the GBGroup.

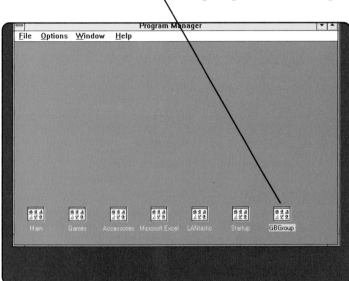

2. **Click twice quickly** on the **group icon** that contains Excel. It will open up to a window. If you are new to Windows, it may take a little time to get the right rhythm on the double-click. Don't worry if the icon jumps around a little when you click on it.

Your group window will have different icons from those you see in this example. The icon for Excel will be the same, however.

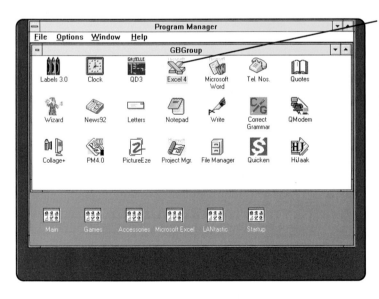

3. **Click twice** on the **Excel icon**. You will see an hourglass, then the copyright information for Excel. If you installed the complete program, the first time you boot up Excel, you will be offered the opportunity to try the on-line tutorial.

ON-LINE TUTORIAL OPTIONS

The first time you open Excel is the *only* time the tutorial option will be presented to you automatically. You have two options at this point:

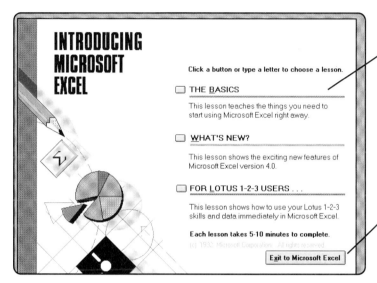

❖ **Click** on the appropriate **topic** to go through a tutorial. Follow the directions on the screen. When you exit the tutorial, you will see a blank worksheet like the one shown on the next page.

❖ **Click** on **Exit to Microsoft Excel** if you do not want to go through a tutorial at this time. A blank worksheet like the one shown on the next page will appear on your screen.

Calling Up the Tutorial

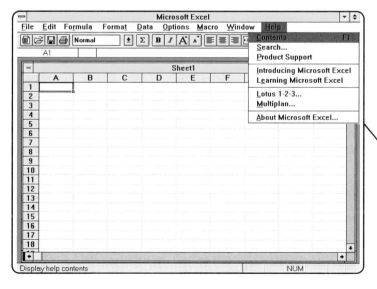

You can open a tutorial at any time with the following steps:

1. **Click** on **Help** in the menu bar. A pull-down menu will appear that lists the tutorials.

2. **Click** on the **tutorial** you would like to use. It will appear on your screen.

THE EXCEL WORKSHEET

This is the standard opening screen in Excel.

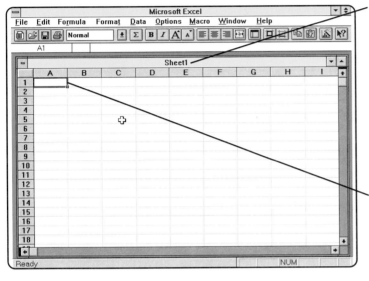

Notice that the worksheet is labeled "Sheet1." This will change when you name the file.

A worksheet is made up of *columns* and *rows*. The intersection of a column and a row forms a block, or *cell*.

The selection border around the first cell on the worksheet tells you that this is the *active,* or *current,* cell. This is the cell that will be affected by the next entry or command.

The *cell reference* in the upper-left portion of your screen also tells you which cell has been selected to receive the next entry or command. The cell reference is A1 because the selected cell is located in column A, row 1.

Notice the mouse pointer has a plus-sign shape when it is in the worksheet area. The pointer changes shape depending on its location and the action you are performing.

ENTERING A WORKSHEET TITLE

When you create a worksheet, it's a good idea to enter a title. Once the worksheet is printed, the worksheet title will enable you (and others who look at the worksheet) to know what the subject is.

1. **Click** on cell **A1** to select it. (On your screen it will be blank.) If it has a border, it is already selected and you don't need to click on it. (It will do no harm if you do, however.)

2. **Type** the word **Sales**. The letters will appear in the cell and in the *formula bar,* which displays characters as you type. If you make a typing error, just **press** the **Backspace** key and retype.

When you begin to type, notice than an ✕ (the *Cancel box*) and a ✔ (the *Enter box*) appear in the formula bar.

3. **Click** on ✔ to confirm that you want to enter "Sales" into A1. The mouse pointer changes to an arrow when it points to the Enter box. The Cancel and Enter boxes will disappear after you confirm the entry.

ENTERING COLUMN HEADINGS

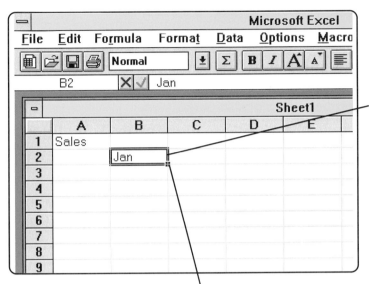

In this section you will enter the abbreviation for January as the heading for column B.

1. **Click** on **B2**. On your screen it will be blank.

2. **Type Jan**.

3. **Press** the **Enter key** on your **keyboard**. (This does the same thing as clicking on the ✔.)

Note the small square in the lower-right corner of the selection border. This is called a *fill handle*. You will use the fill handle in the next section.

USING THE AUTOFILL FEATURE TO COMPLETE A SERIES

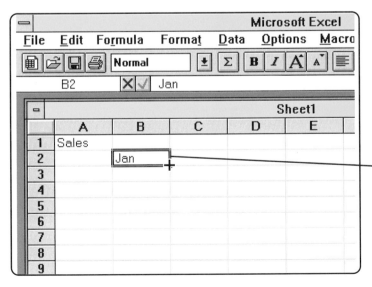

Once you have typed the first name in a common series (such as months in the year or days in the week), you can use the AutoFill feature to complete the series.

1. **Move** the mouse pointer to the **fill handle**. It will change to a black plus sign. You may have to fiddle with the pointer to get it to change shape.

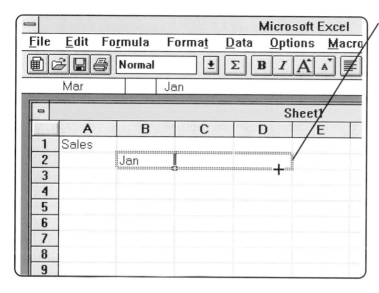

2. **Press and hold** the mouse button as you **drag** the fill handle **across columns C** and **D**. The border of the cell will expand as you drag.

3. **Release** the button. The AutoFill feature will automatically complete the series for you as you can see in the next example.

If you want to include six months in the series, simply drag the fill handle across columns E, F, and G. Notice that February and March appeared as abbreviations. If you had typed "January," the succeeding months also would have been spelled out in full.

If you mistakenly fill in more cells in the series than you want, simply drag the fill handle backwards to erase the unwanted names.

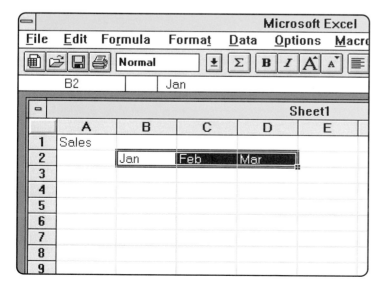

You can also drag the fill handle down the worksheet to create a series in a column format. It's quite an amazing feature!

You can generate a series of numbers by typing the *first two* numbers in the sequence. You can also use the AutoFill feature to repeat the contents of a cell across many cells.

ENTERING ROW HEADINGS

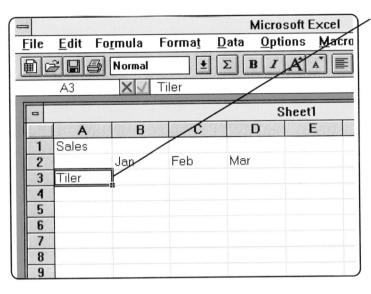

1. **Click** on **A3**. On your screen the cell will be blank.

2. **Type** the name **Tiler**.

3. **Press Enter.**

4. **Click** on **A4**. On your screen it will be blank.

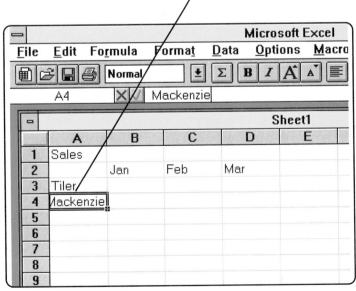

5. **Type** the name **Mackenzie**. Notice that the name is too long for the column and the "M" is beginning to move backwards. It's okay. You'll fix it once all the names are typed.

6. **Press Enter.** Notice that the name extends slightly into the next column.

7. **Click** on **A5**. On your screen it will be blank.

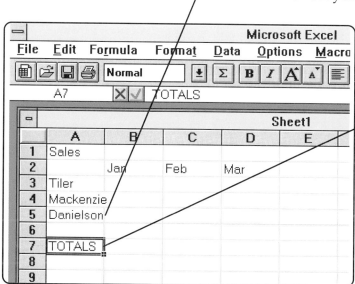

8. **Type** the name **Danielson**.

9. **Press Enter.**

10. **Click** on **A7**. On your screen it will be blank.

11. **Type TOTALS**.

12. **Press Enter.**

Your worksheet will look like the example to the left.

CHANGING COLUMN WIDTH

In this section you will change the width of column A to accommodate the long name. You'll love the ease with which this happens.

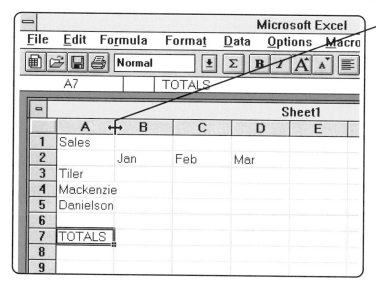

1. **Move** the mouse pointer up to the **line between columns A** and **B**. The pointer will change shape.

2. Click twice. The column will be expanded to a "best fit" width that will take into account the longest entry in the column. (Don't you love it?!) If nothing happens, try a faster speed on the double-clicks.

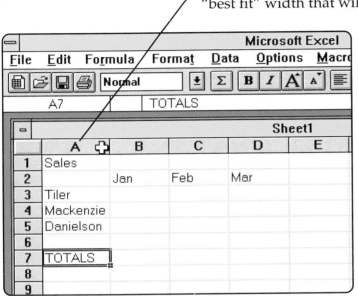

SORTING DATA ALPHABETICALLY

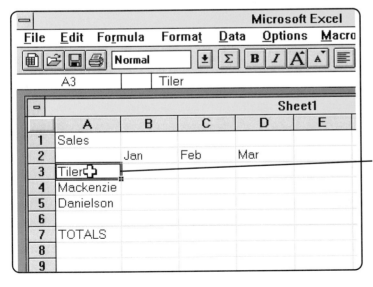

The ability to sort data after it has been entered into the worksheet is a helpful feature of Excel. In this section you will sort the names in column A alphabetically.

1. Click on **A3** and leave the pointer in the middle of the cell. Make sure the pointer looks like a white plus sign.

2. **Press and hold** the mouse button and **drag** the pointer down to **A5**.

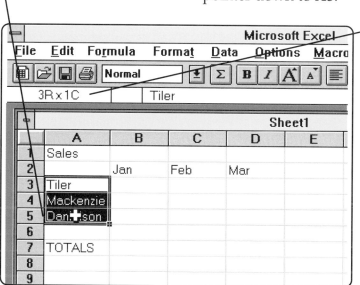

Notice that the cell reference area indicates that you have highlighted three rows in one column (3Rx1C). This is called a *range* because the cells are adjacent, or next to each other.

3. **Release** the mouse button when you have highlighted the range A3 through A5.

Notice that the range is highlighted in black except for the first cell, which remains white to tell you that this is the active cell.

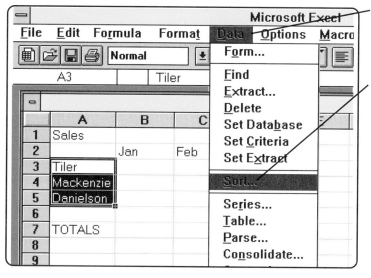

4. **Click** on **Data** in the menu bar. A pull-down menu will appear.

5. **Click** on **Sort**. Three dots (called an *ellipsis*) after a choice indicate that selecting this choice will bring up a dialog box that will ask for additional information. In this case the Sort dialog box will appear. It's all right if the dialog box appears in a different spot on the screen than the one in the next example.

6. **Click** on **Rows** if it does not already have a black dot in the circle (called an *option button* in Windows terminology).

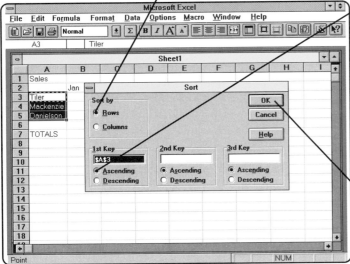

7. **Click** on **Ascending** if it does not already have a dot in the circle.

Ascending order means from A to Z (or 1 to *n* for numbers). *Descending* order means from Z to A (or *n* to 1 for numbers).

8. **Click** on **OK**. The dialog box will disappear.

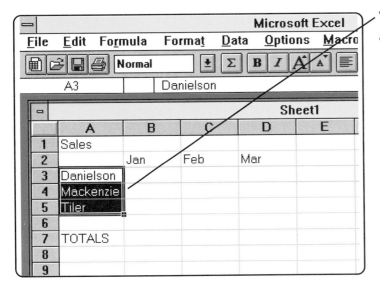

The names are now sorted alphabetically.

ENTERING NUMBERS

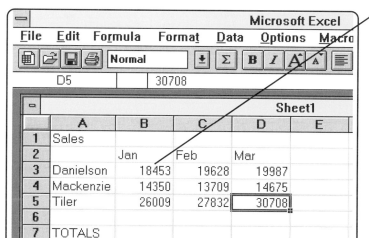

1. **Click** on **B3**. On your screen the cell will be empty.

2. **Type** the number **18453**.

3. **Press** ↓ (the Down Arrow key on your keyboard) to enter the number into B3 and automatically move the selection border to B4. Using the arrow keys on your keyboard is another way to enter data and move around the worksheet. (If you are using the arrows on the numeric keyboard, make sure Num Lock is off.)

4. **Enter** the **numbers** shown on the screen above in the appropriate cells on your worksheet.

Remember, there are several ways to confirm that you want to enter data into the worksheet:

❖ Click on ✔

❖ Press Enter

❖ Press an arrow key on your keyboard to enter the data and to move the selection border to the next cell in the direction of the arrow

Notice that numbers are automatically aligned on the right in a cell. Text is aligned on the left.

This worksheet will be used throughout the rest of the book. In Chapter 2, "Editing Your Worksheet," you will make corrections to it.

Editing Your Worksheet

Editing is straightforward in Excel. Using the mouse gives you a great deal of control in the editing process. You can change the contents of a cell, change individual letters or numbers in a cell, clear a cell completely, or even undo your edit if you change your mind. In this chapter you will:

❖ Make edits to the worksheet you created in Chapter 1 so that you can use the worksheet throughout the rest of this book

❖ Learn to use the Undo option

ADDING DATA

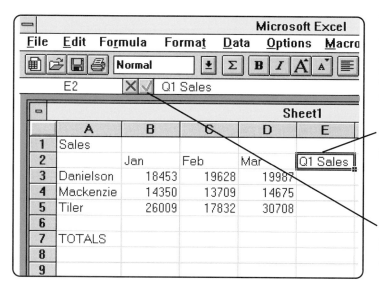

You can add data at any time to a worksheet. In this section you will add the heading "Q1 Sales" to column E.

1. **Click** on **E2**. On your screen it will be blank.

2. **Type Q1 Sales**.

3. **Click** on ✔ (the Enter box) to confirm that you want to enter Q1 Sales in E2.

INSERTING A CHARACTER INTO A CELL

In this section you will change the name "Tiler" to "Tiller."

1. Click on Tiler in **A5**. A selection border will appear around the cell and Tiler will appear in the formula bar.

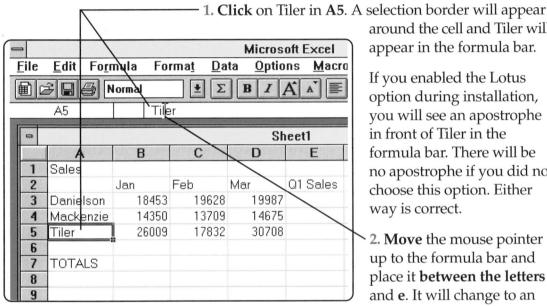

If you enabled the Lotus option during installation, you will see an apostrophe in front of Tiler in the formula bar. There will be no apostrophe if you did not choose this option. Either way is correct.

2. Move the mouse pointer up to the formula bar and place it **between the letters l** and **e**. It will change to an I-beam.

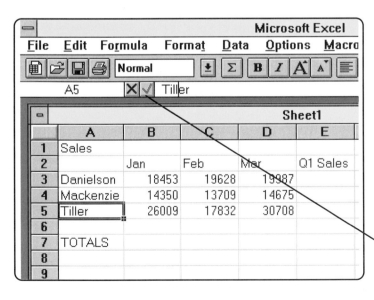

3. Click to set the cursor in place. It will change to a flashing bar. If the bar is not where you want it, press → or ← until it is positioned correctly. (If you are using the numeric keypad, make sure Num Lock is off.)

4. Type the letter l. It will be added to the name.

5. Click on ✔.

DELETING A CHARACTER FROM A CELL

In this section you will change the name "Mackenzie" to "McKenzie."

Deleting to the Right

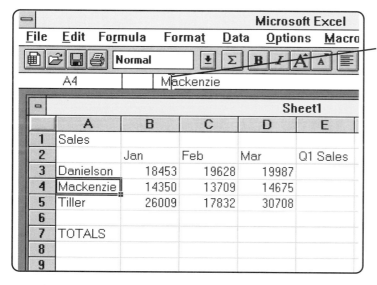

1. **Click** on Mackenzie in **A4**.

2. **Move** the mouse pointer up to the formula bar and place it to the **left of** the letter **a**. The cursor will change to an I-beam.

3. **Click** to set the cursor in place. It will change to a flashing bar.

4. **Press** the **Del** key to delete the letter "a."

Deleting to the Left

1. **Press** → **twice** to move the flashing bar to the right of the letter "k."

2. **Press** the **Backspace** key to delete the "k."

3. **Type** a capital **K** to make the name McKenzie.

4. **Click** on ✔ to confirm the entry.

DELETING MORE THAN ONE CHARACTER

In this section you will change the name "Danielson" to "Daniels."

1. **Click** on Danielson in **A3**.

2. **Move** the mouse pointer up to the formula bar and place it to the **right of** the last letter of the word. The pointer will change to an I-beam.

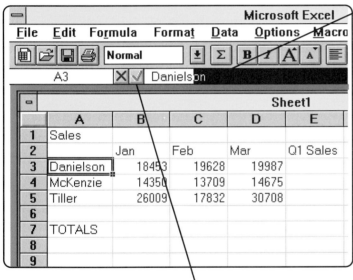

3. **Press and hold** the mouse button as you **drag** the pointer over the **last two letters** in the name. A black highlight bar will cover the letters and the empty part of the formula bar.

4. **Release** the mouse button.

5. **Press Backspace** to delete the letters.

6. **Click** on ✔ to confirm the change.

UNDOING AN EDIT

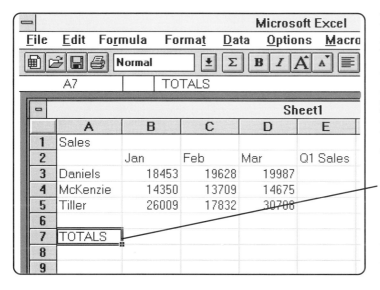

Excel has a wonderfully forgiving feature called Undo that allows you to undo a change you have just made. In this section you will clear the contents of a cell and then undo that change.

1. **Click** on TOTALS in **A7**.

2. **Press Backspace**. The contents of the cell will be cleared.

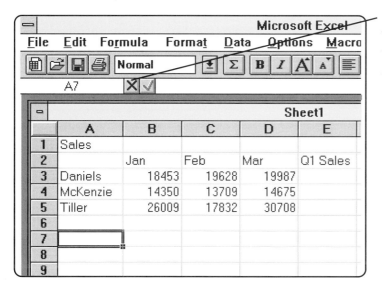

3. **Click** on ✕ (the Cancel box) to undo the change. You can also press Esc to undo, or reverse, the edit.

Totaling Columns and Rows

This is the fun part! Excel has a wonderful shortcut, called the AutoSum tool, that contains a built-in formula to total columns and rows. You can then use another feature, called AutoFill, to copy the addition formula to other cells. In this chapter you will:

❖ Use the AutoSum tool to total columns and rows

❖ Use the AutoFill feature to copy the addition formula to other cells

USING THE AUTOSUM TOOL

Although you can write a formula to total a column or row, clicking on the AutoSum tool creates the formula for you automatically. (You will learn how to write formulas in Chapter 13, "Writing Formulas.")

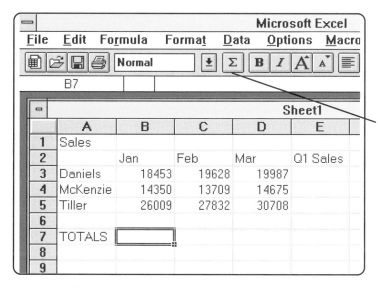

Totaling a Column

1. **Click** on **B7**.

2. **Click** on the **AutoSum tool** in the toolbar. (Σ is the Greek symbol for sum.) A moving border will surround the numbers in column B. The formula for summing the column, SUM(B3:B6), will appear in B7 and in the formula bar.

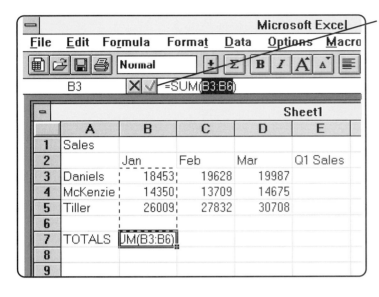

3. Click on ✔ to confirm the entry. The sum of column B will appear in B7.

Don't get carried away and add columns C and D just yet. You will learn how to copy the sum formula to other columns a little later in the chapter.

You can use these same procedures to total a row.

Totaling a Row

1. Click on **E3**. On your screen it will be blank.

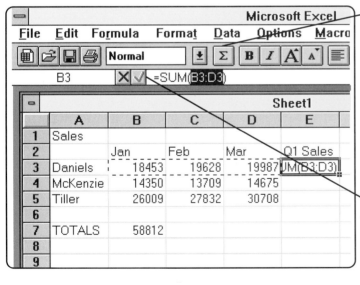

2. Click on the **AutoSum tool** in the toolbar. A moving border will surround the numbers in row 3. The formula for totaling the row, SUM(B3:D3), will appear in the formula bar and in the cell.

3. Click on ✔ to confirm the entry. The sum of row 3 will appear in E3.

Now you're ready to copy the sum formula to other columns and rows.

COPYING A FORMULA

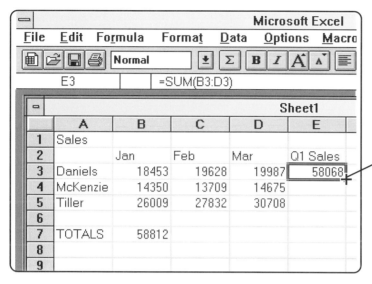

In this section you will copy the formula that totaled row 3 so that it will total rows 4 and 5.

1. **Click** on **E3** if it is not already selected.

2. **Move** the mouse pointer to the fill handle in the lower-right corner of the selection border. It will change to a black plus sign.

3. **Press and hold** the mouse button and **drag** the fill handle down to **E4 and E5**. The cell border will expand to surround all three cells.

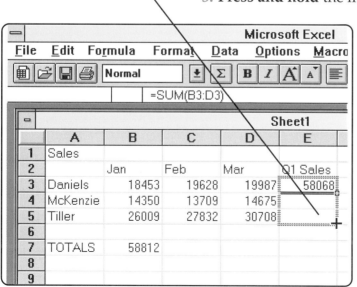

4. **Release** the mouse button and the sums will appear in E4 and E5.

Do not extend the cell border down to E7. Since there are no numbers in row 6 to total, the formula will put a 0 in cell E6. You will include E7 in the next step.

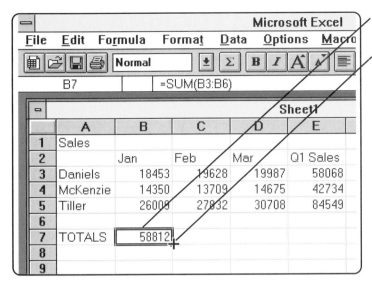

5. Click on **B7**.

6. Move the mouse pointer to the fill handle in the lower-right corner of the selection border. It will change to a black plus sign.

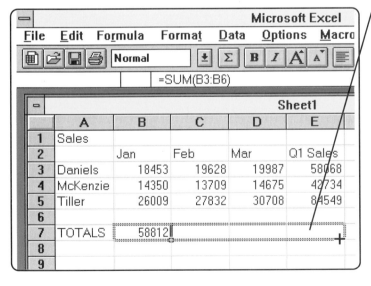

7. Press and hold the mouse button and **drag** the fill handle over to **E7**.

8. Release the button and the following sums will appear:

Column C = 61169

Column D = 65370

Column E = 185351

You will save this file in Chapter 4, "Naming and Saving Files."

Naming and Saving Files

Since Excel is a Windows-based program, it uses standard Windows commands to name and save files. In this chapter you will:

❖ Name a file using the Save As command

❖ Learn two ways to save a file

NAMING A FILE

Use the Save As command to name a file. You can have up to eight characters in the name. Excel will automatically add the .XLS extension to identify this as a worksheet file.

1. Click on **File** in the menu bar. A pull-down menu will appear.

2. Click on **Save As**. The Save As dialog box will appear. It may appear in a different spot on your screen than you see in the next example.

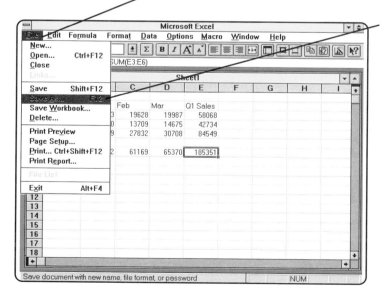

Since Sheet1 in the File Name text box is already high-lighted, you can simply begin to type the new filename.

3. **Type salesq1**. (Filenames are not allowed to have spaces). It will replace the highlighted text.

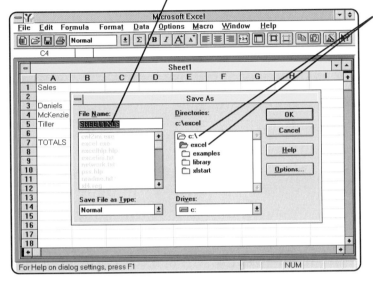

The open file folders next to "c:\" and "excel" indicate that the file will be saved on the C drive in the Excel directory.

It doesn't matter if you type the filename in capital or small letters. The filename will appear in capital letters on the worksheet. Excel will automatically add the .XLS extension to identify it as a worksheet.

SAVING A FILE

Develop the habit of saving your file while you work on it. Save often. This will spare you much grief and aggravation in the event of a power failure or equipment problem.

With the Save File tool you can save with a click of your mouse.

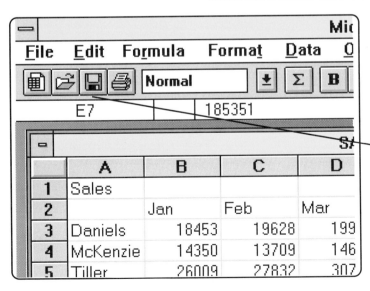

1. **Click** on the **Save File tool** in the toolbar. You won't see any difference in your screen, but your worksheet is saved. Do this often.

Printing Files and Using Help

When you print an Excel file you can customize the printed page in a number of ways. You can add identifying information to a file with headers and footers. You can preview a file to see what it will look like when it prints. There are so many features that can be customized that you may find this a good time to use the Help feature of Excel. In this chapter you will:

❖ Add a header and erase a footer from the file

❖ Center the worksheet on the printed page and preview the page before you print

❖ Learn to use the Help feature

❖ Print the worksheet with extra large type

THE PRINT TOOL SHORTCUT

1. Click on the **Print tool** in the toolbar. You will see a Printing message box saying that the file is now printing. Click on Cancel in the message box if you want to cancel the print command. Since the file is short, the message box will appear only briefly. It will be on the screen for a longer time for a longer file.

	Microsoft Excel
File Edit Formula Format Data Options Macro	

| | Normal | ↓ | Σ | **B** | *I* | **A** | A⁻ | ≡ |

E7 | 185351

			SALESQ1.XLS

	A	B	C	D	E
1	Sales				
2		Jan	Feb	Mar	Q1 Sales
3	Daniels	18453	19628	19987	58068
4	McKenzie	14350	13709	14675	42734
5	Tiller	26009	27832	30708	84549
6					
7	TOTALS	58812	61169	65370	185351
8					
9					

When you use the Print tool, the file will print according to the specifications included in the Page Setup dialog box. You can change any or all of these specifications, as shown in the next sections.

OPENING THE PAGE SETUP DIALOG BOX

You can customize everything about printing an Excel file through the Page Setup dialog box. The settings you make in this dialog box affect only this particular file.

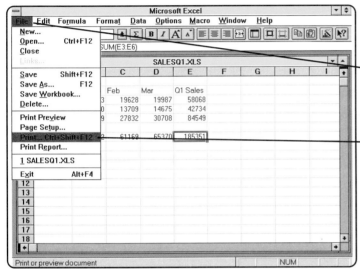

1. **Click** on **File** in the menu bar. A pull-down menu will appear.

2. **Click** on **Print**. The Print dialog box will appear. You can also click directly on Page Setup. The Print dialog box gives you access to both the Page Setup and the Print Preview options.

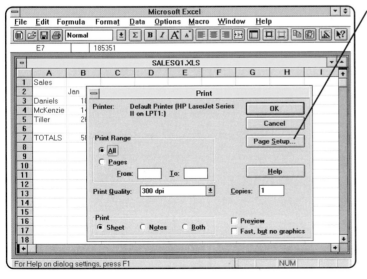

3. **Click** on **Page Setup**. The Page Setup dialog box will appear.

Notice the message at the bottom of your screen. The message changes to reflect the task you are doing and may provide helpful information on completing the task.

REMOVING GRIDLINES FROM THE PRINTED PAGE

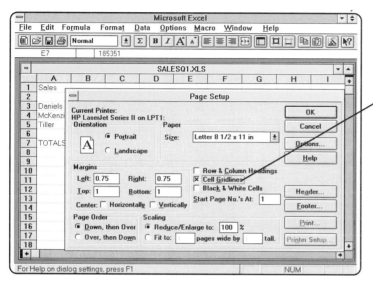

Your page will print with the same gridlines you see on your screen unless you remove them.

1. **Click** on **Cell Gridlines** to *remove* the ✕ from the box. If you leave the ✕ in the box, the worksheet will print with gridlines on it. Removing the gridlines from the printed page will not affect the gridlines on your screen.

WORKING WITH HEADERS AND FOOTERS

In Excel, you can add text to the top or bottom of the printed page, as shown in the next two sections.

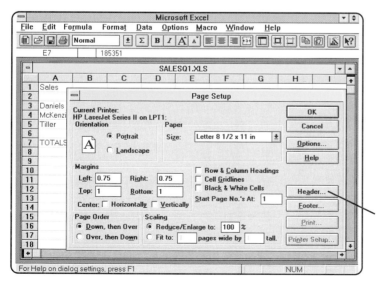

Creating a Header

A *header* is a line of type that is added to the top of the printed page. It usually contains identifying data, such as the filename or the date, but it can be any text you want.

1. **Click** on **Header** in the Page Setup dialog box. The Header dialog box will appear.

2. Place the cursor **after &F** in the Center Section box and **click** to set the cursor in place. (&F is the code to insert the filename.)

Header material typed in the Center Section box will be printed in the center at the top of the page. Header material typed in the Left and Right Section boxes will be printed at the top left and right margins, respectively.

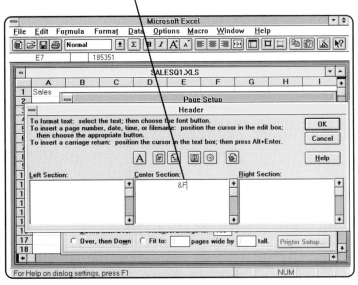

The buttons in the Header dialog box and their functions are:

Ⓐ Displays Font dialog box

⊞ Inserts page number

⊞ Inserts total number of pages

⊞ Inserts current date

⊗ Inserts current time

⑤ Inserts filename

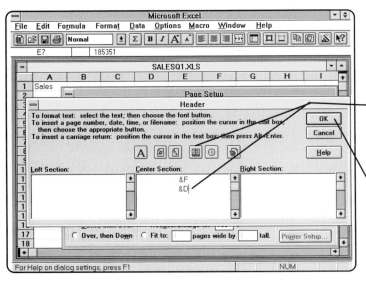

3. Press and hold Alt then **press Enter** (Alt + Enter) to move the pointer to the next line.

4. Click on the **Date button** to insert the current date. The &D code will appear.

5. Click on **OK** to confirm the change and close the Header dialog box. The Page Setup dialog box will be on your screen.

Erasing a Footer

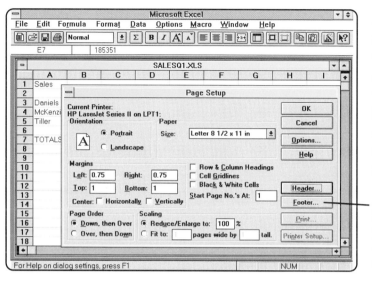

A *footer* is a line of type that is added to the bottom of the printed page. Excel is set up to print "Page" plus the page number at the bottom of the page automatically. In this section you will remove the footer notation.

1. **Click** on **Footer** in the Page Setup dialog box. The Footer dialog box will appear.

2. **Place** the cursor **after Page &P** in the Center Section box and **click** to set the cursor in place.

3. **Press and hold** the mouse button as you **drag** the cursor over the **page number code**. It will be highlighted by a dark bar.

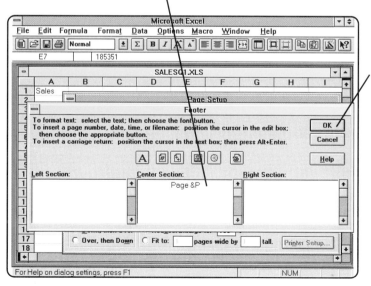

4. **Press Backspace** to delete the code.

5. **Click** on **OK** to confirm the change. Or, click on Cancel if you don't want to remove the footer. The Footer dialog box will close and the Page Setup dialog box will be on your screen.

PRINTING WITH LARGE TYPE

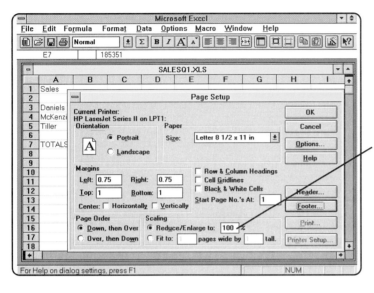

You can significantly enlarge the size of the type on the printed page. This is especially helpful if you plan to use the page in a presentation.

1. **Click** to set the cursor to the right of "100" in the Reduce/Enlarge to text box.

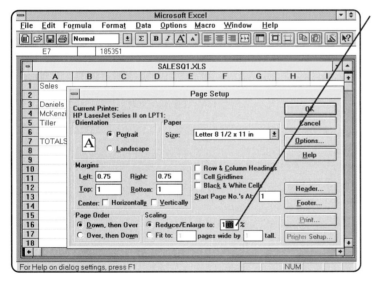

2. **Press and hold** the mouse button and **drag** the cursor over the **00** in 100. It will be highlighted. **Release** the mouse button.

3. **Type 50** to make the enlargement factor 150%. You can use this big an enlargement factor because the SalesQ1 worksheet does not contain a great deal of data. Experiment with different sizes. If you want a smaller print than normal, type a number less than 100. (This affects the printout only. To change the size of the type on your printout *and* on the screen, see "Increasing Type Size" in Chapter 9.)

CENTERING THE WORKSHEET ON THE PRINTED PAGE

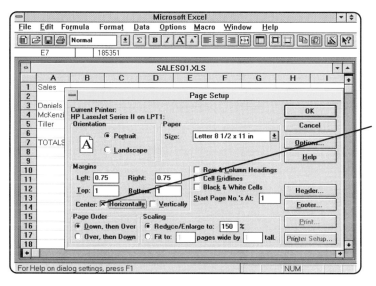

You can center the worksheet across the page (horizontally) and/or up and down the page (vertically).

1. **Click** on **Horizontally** to insert an X in the box.

USING HELP

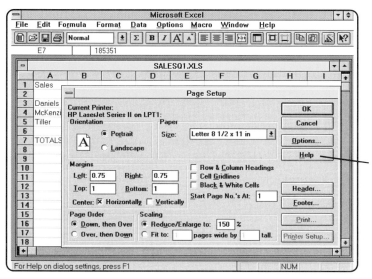

There is a Help button in every dialog box. Simply clicking on the Help button gives you access to an encyclopedia of information about the elements in the dialog box.

1. **Click** on **Help**. After a brief pause the Microsoft Excel Help dialog box will appear.

2. Click on ↓ in the vertical scroll bar to scroll through the list of elements in the dialog box.

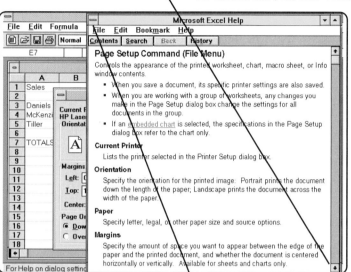

3. Click twice on the **Control menu box** (⊟) on the left of the Help title bar. This will close the Help dialog box. The Page Setup dialog box will be on your screen.

CLOSING THE PAGE SETUP DIALOG BOX

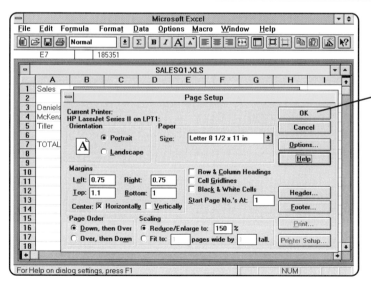

You are almost ready to print your edited worksheet.

1. Click on **OK** to save all the settings you made and close the Page Setup dialog box.

PREVIEWING THE PAGE

The Preview screen lets you see the placement of the worksheet on the page and make changes before you print.

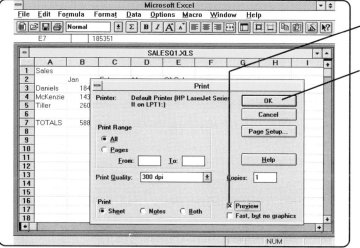

1. **Click** on **Preview** to insert an X in the box.

2. **Click** on **OK** to confirm the change and close the dialog box. The Preview screen for SALESQ1.XLS will appear on your screen.

The Preview screen will now appear every time you print a file, even when you print with the Print tool. If you don't select the Preview option, you can still see a Preview screen if you:

❖ Click on File in the menu bar, then click on Print Preview in the pull-down menu

❖ Or, press and hold the Shift key while you click on the Print tool in the toolbar

Using the Zoom Feature

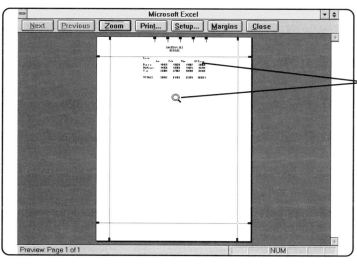

In the Preview screen the pointer looks like a magnifying glass.

1. **Place** the magnifying glass over the worksheet area.

2. **Click** the mouse button. The area you selected will be enlarged.

3. **Click** the mouse button again to return to the full-page view.

Changing Margins Through the Preview Screen

You can change the margin settings through the Page Setup dialog box. You can also change the margins through the Preview screen. In this section you will increase the top margin.

1. If your preview page does not show the margin lines, **click** on the **Margins button** at the top of the Preview screen.

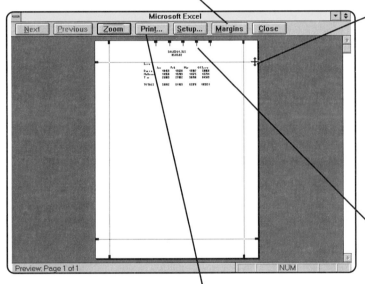

2. Place the pointer on the **handle** on the **top margin**. The pointer will change shape.

3. Press and hold the mouse button as you **drag** the line down an **inch** or so. This will increase the top margin.

You can change the column widths by dragging the column handles.

4. Click on **Print** to print the document. The Print dialog box will appear. Or, **click** on **Close** to close the Preview screen without printing.

Closing a File and Exiting Excel

In Windows-based programs you can often accomplish the same task several different ways. Excel is no exception. In this chapter you will:

❖ Learn a quick way to close a file
❖ Learn a quick way to exit Excel

CLOSING A FILE

When you close a file, you do not exit Excel. A new Sheet1 appears on your screen.

1. Click twice on the **Control menu box** (⊟) on the left of the SALESQ1.XLS title bar. If you saved just prior to doing this, the SALESQ1.XLS file will close and a new Sheet1 will be on your screen.

If you did not save before clicking on the Control menu box, a dialog box will appear and ask if you want to save.

2. Click on **Yes**.

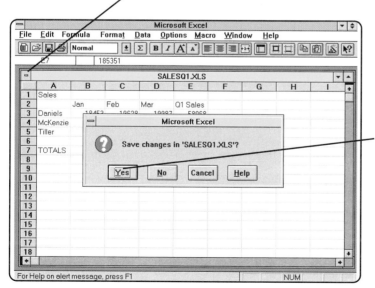

EXITING EXCEL

If you have been following along with the steps in this chapter, you closed the SALESQ1 worksheet and you have a blank Sheet1 on your screen. If you did not close the file on your screen, this exit procedure will work anyway.

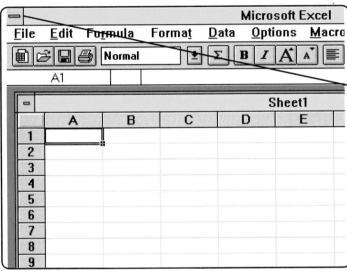

1. **Click twice** on the **Control menu box** (⊟) on the left of the Microsoft Excel title bar. If you saved before doing this, Excel will close.

If you forgot to save, Excel will rescue you and ask if you want to save.

2. **Click** on **Yes** to save and exit Excel.

Program Manager

Part II: Adding Style to Your Worksheet

Opening a Saved File

Excel has a special tool that makes opening a saved file as easy as clicking your mouse. And, amazingly, Excel even has a shortcut for that. In this chapter you will:

❖ Learn two ways to open the SALESQ1.XLS file

OPENING A SAVED FILE

Excel has added a special feature to the File pull-down menu that makes opening a saved file especially easy.

Method #1

1. If you are not in Excel, **click twice** on the **Excel icon** on your screen to load the program. A blank Sheet1 will appear on your screen when the program is loaded.

2. **Click** on **File** in the menu bar. A pull-down menu will appear.

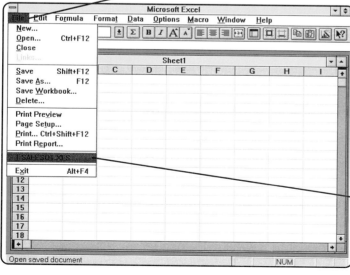

The File pull-down menu lists the four most recent files you have opened. As you create files, the list will change. In this example, SALESQ1.XLS is the only file on the pull-down menu.

3. **Click** on **SALESQ1.XLS**. The worksheet will appear on your screen.

43

Method #2

If you want to follow along with these steps, close the SALESQ1 worksheet you opened with Method #1.

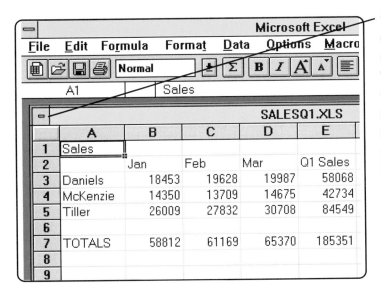

1. **Click twice** on the **Control menu box** (⊟) in the SALESQ1.XLS title bar. The SALESQ1 worksheet will close and a blank Sheet1 will appear on your screen. This is the screen you see when you boot up Excel.

2. **Click** on the **Open File tool** in the toolbar.

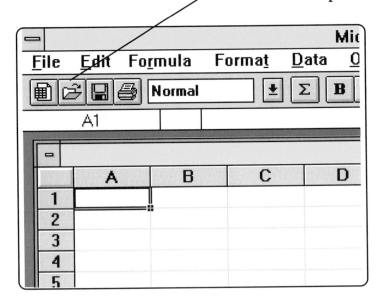

The Open dialog box will appear on your screen. It may appear in a different spot than you see in the next example.

3. **Click twice** on **SALESQ1.XLS**. You will briefly see an hourglass as Excel loads the file.

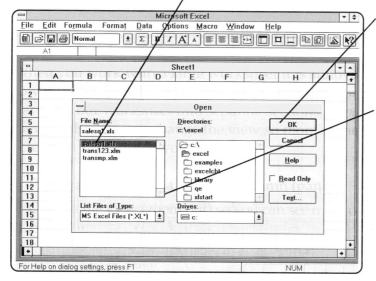

You can also **click once** on the **filename** and then **click** on **OK** to open the file.

If there are many files in the list, click on the ↓ on the scroll bar until the file you want comes into view. Then click twice on it.

Adding and Deleting Rows with a Shortcut Menu

As part of the process of adding and deleting rows, you will use one of the new features of Excel called a shortcut menu. If you think that clicking on the menu bar and getting a pull-down menu is easy, just wait until you use a shortcut menu! In this chapter you will:

❖ Add rows

❖ Delete a row

❖ Use the shortcut menu

ADDING ROWS

Suppose you want the company name on the SALESQ1 worksheet for a presentation tomorrow. In this section you will add three rows at the beginning of the SALESQ1 worksheet in order to add the company name. You will also add some other blank rows within the worksheet.

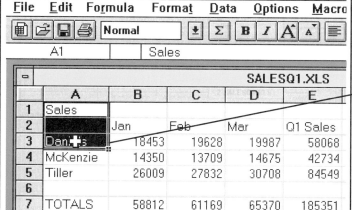

1. **Click** on Sales in **A1**. Leave the pointer in the cell.

2. **Press and hold** the mouse button and **drag** the pointer down to **A3**.

3. **Release** the mouse button when you have highlighted A1 through A3. Leave the pointer in A3.

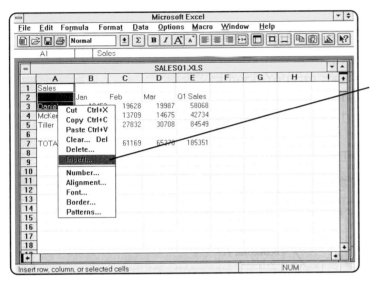

4. Press the **right mouse button**. A shortcut menu will appear.

5. Click on **Insert**. The Insert dialog box will appear.

6. Click on **Entire Row** to put a black dot in the circle.

7. Click on **OK**. The dialog box will disappear and three rows will be added where you highlighted.

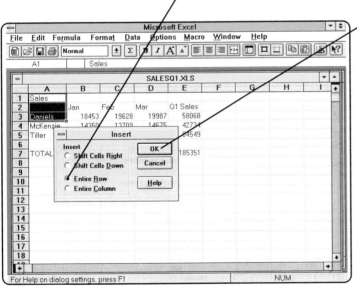

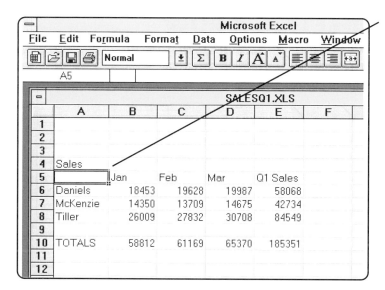

8. **Click** on **A5** and leave the pointer in the cell. **Follow steps 4 through 7** to add a blank row above "Jan."

9. **Click** on Daniels in **A7**. Leave the pointer in the cell. **Follow steps 4 through 7** again to add a blank row between the months and the sales figures.

DELETING A ROW

After looking at your worksheet you decide that three rows at the top are too many. Don't worry. Deleting is easy.

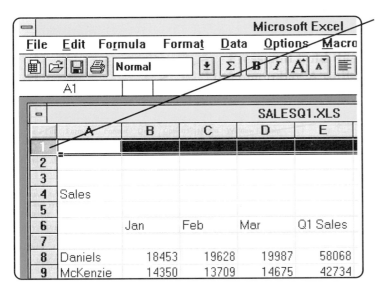

1. **Click** on the **Row 1 button**. This will select the entire row. Leave the pointer in A1.

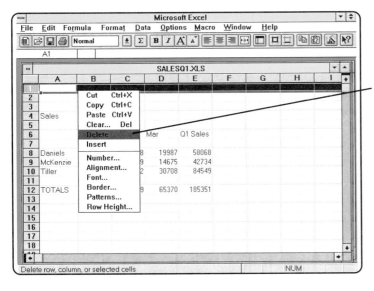

2. **Press** the **right mouse button**. A shortcut menu will appear.

3. **Click** on **Delete**. The row you highlighted will be deleted and its number assigned to the next row.

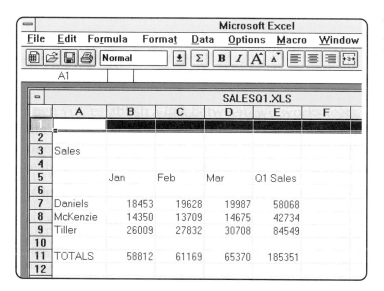

Your worksheet will look like this example.

ADDING A WORKSHEET HEADING

In this section you will add the company name to the worksheet and change "Sales" to a more descriptive heading.

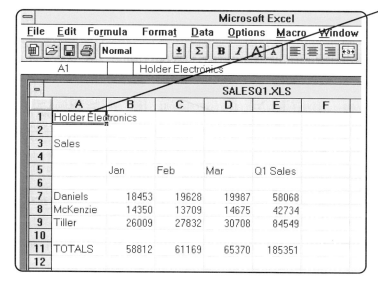

1. **Click** on **A1**. On your screen the cell will be empty.

2. **Type Holder Electronics**.

3. **Press Enter** to insert the name into A1.

Don't be concerned about the name being too long for the cell. You will center the company name over the worksheet in "Centering Across Columns and Within Cells" in Chapter 9.

4. **Click** on Sales in **A3**.

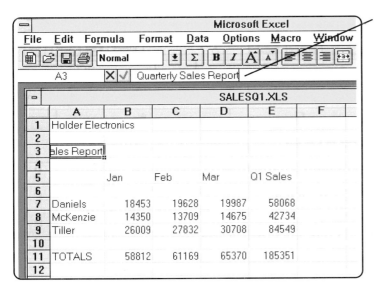

5. **Type** the words **Quarterly Sales Report**. They will replace "Sales."

6. **Press Enter** to insert "Quarterly Sales Report" in A3.

7. **Click** on the **Save File tool** in the toolbar to save the changes you made to your worksheet.

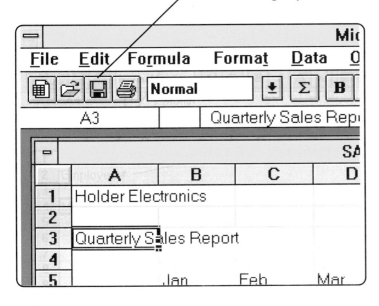

In the next chapter you will dress up the worksheet with larger type, boldface print, and other style changes.

Changing Type Styles and Centering Text

The toolbar you see on your screen is called the Standard toolbar. It contains tools for the most commonly performed tasks. Excel also has a collection of specialized toolbars. One of these toolbars, the Formatting toolbar, contains tools to help you improve the appearance of your worksheet. In this chapter you will:

❖ Call up the Formatting toolbar and change its position on your screen

❖ Learn two ways to increase type size

❖ Change type style to bold and italics

❖ Underline text

❖ Center the heading over a worksheet

OPENING THE FORMATTING TOOLBAR

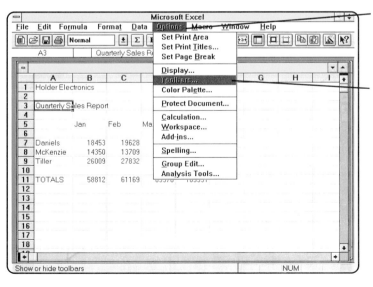

1. **Click** on **Options** in the menu bar. A pull-down menu will appear.

2. **Click** on **Toolbars**. The Toolbars dialog box will appear.

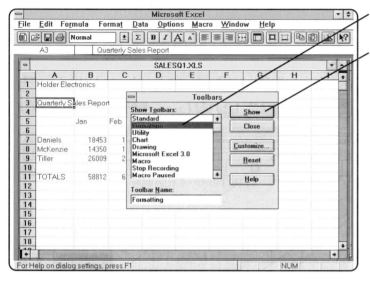

3. Click on **Formatting**.

4. Click on **Show**. The Formatting toolbox will appear. It may be in a different spot or even in a different shape than you see in the next example.

CHANGING THE POSITION OF A TOOLBAR

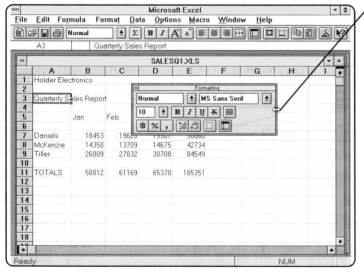

1. Move the mouse pointer to the **right edge of the Formatting toolbox**. The pointer will change to a two-headed arrow. It may take a little fiddling to get the pointer to change shape.

2. Press and hold the mouse button and **drag** the two-headed arrow to the **far right** of the worksheet. You will see an outline shape expand to the right as you drag.

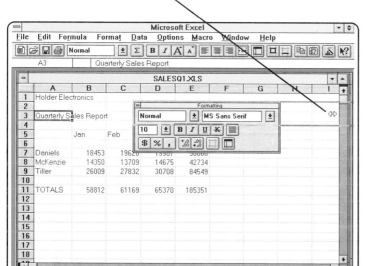

3. Release the mouse button at the far right of the worksheet. The toolbox will change into a toolbar.

Don't be concerned that it covers part of the worksheet. You will move it in step 4.

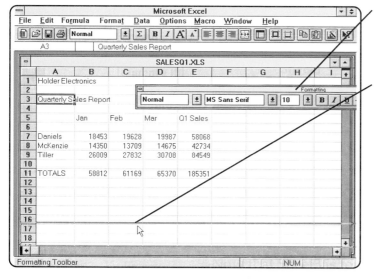

4. Place the mouse pointer beside **"Formatting"** in the **title bar** of the toolbar.

5. Press and hold the mouse button and **drag** the toolbar outline to the **bottom** of the worksheet.

6. Release the mouse button when the outline is centered across the bottom of the worksheet. The toolbar will appear in place of the outline.

INCREASING TYPE SIZE

There are two ways to increase type size. Method #1 uses the Formatting toolbar. Method #2 uses the Standard toolbar.

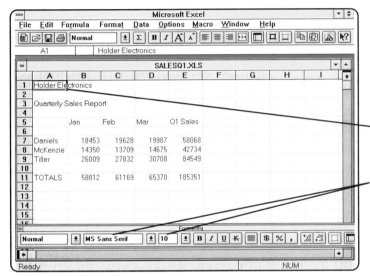

Method #1

1. Click on Holder Electronics in **A1**.

The Formatting toolbar shows MS Sans Serif as the font and the type size as 10 points. These are the standard (*default*) settings in Excel. Your settings may be different if someone changed the defaults.

2. Click on ↓ next to the Type Size box. A pop-up list box will appear.

3. Click on **14** to increase the type size of the selected text to 14 points. You will see the change almost immediately on your screen.

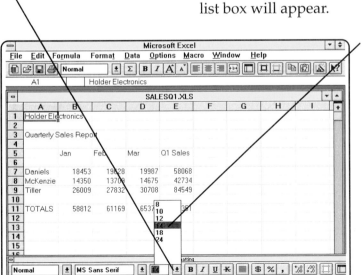

Method #2

1. **Click** on Quarterly Sales Report in **A3**.

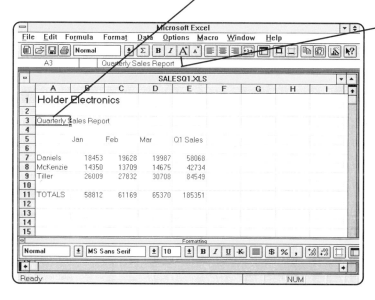

2. **Click** on the **Increase Font Size tool** (the large A) in the Standard toolbar. This tool increases the font to the next size, which is 12 points. You will see the change almost immediately on your screen.

MAKING TEXT BOLD

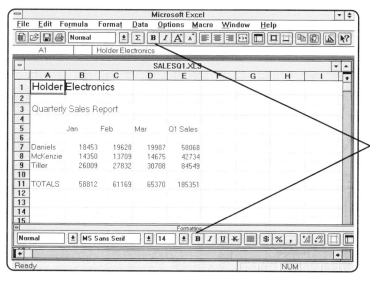

You can further emphasize text by making the type extra dark, or **bold**.

1. **Click** on Holder Electronics in **A1**.

2. **Click** on the **Bold tool** (the large B). Notice there is a Bold tool in the Standard toolbar and in the Formatting toolbar. You can click on either one.

MAKING TEXT ITALIC

In this section you will highlight the text in a series of cells and, with one command, apply italics to all of the cells.

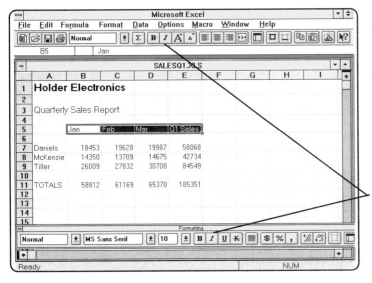

1. **Click** on Jan in **B5**. Leave the pointer in the cell.

2. **Press and hold** the mouse button and **drag** the pointer over to Q1 Sales in **E5**.

3. **Release** the button when you have highlighted B5 through E5.

4. **Click** on one of the **Italics tools** (the large, slanted I). There is one on the Standard toolbar and one on the Formatting toolbar.

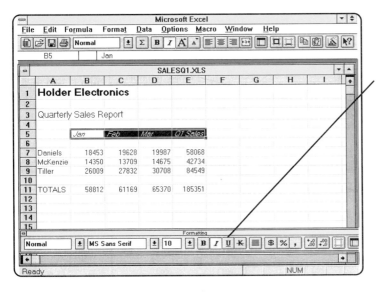

UNDERLINING TEXT

1. **Click** on the **Underline tool** (the large U with the underline) in the Formatting toolbar while the cells are still highlighted.

You may have to click somewhere else on the worksheet in order to see the italics and underlining in cells B5 to E5.

CREATING A
DOUBLE UNDERLINE

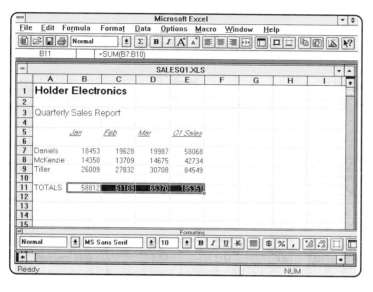

In this section you will put a double underline beneath the totals in row 11.

1. **Click** on **B11**. Leave the pointer in the cell.

2. **Press and hold** the mouse button and **drag** the pointer over to **E11**.

3. **Release** the mouse button when you have highlighted B11 through E11.

4. **Click** on **Format** in the menu bar. A pull-down menu will appear.

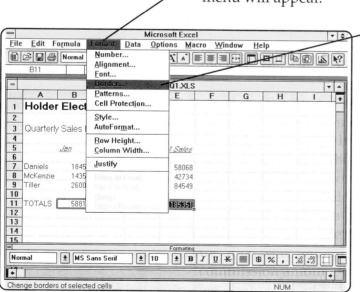

5. **Click** on **Border**. The Border dialog box will appear.

6. **Click** on **Bottom**. A line will appear in the box.

7. **Click** on the **Double Line style box**.

8. **Click** on **OK**. The selected cells will appear with a double underline. You may have to click somewhere else on the worksheet to see the double underline.

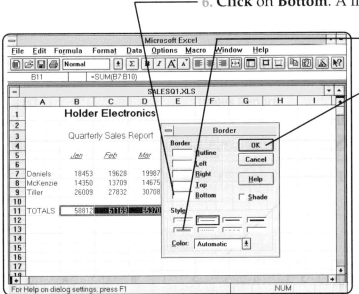

CENTERING ACROSS COLUMNS AND WITHIN CELLS

Text is normally aligned on the left in a cell. In this section, you will highlight rows 1 through 5 and apply the centering option to all of them at the same time.

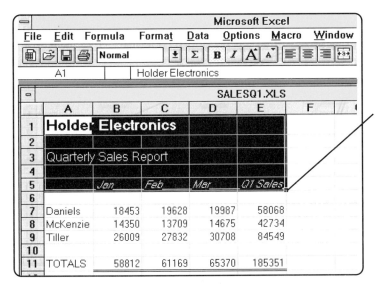

1. **Click** on **A1**. Leave the pointer in the cell.

2. **Press and hold** the mouse button and **drag** the pointer diagonally down to **E5**.

3. **Release** the mouse button when you have highlighted A1 to E5.

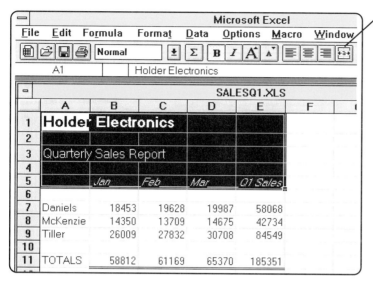

4. Click on the **Center Across Columns tool** in the Standard toolbar. The heading and subheading will be centered across the columns. Each of the column headings in row 5 will be centered within its cell.

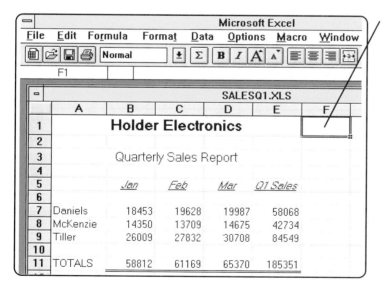

5. Click anywhere else on the worksheet to see the centering. Your worksheet will look like this example.

You will format the numbers on the worksheet in the next chapter.

Formatting Numbers

The standard format for numbers is called the General number format. In this format, if you want a comma or a decimal in your number you must enter it that way. You can change the General format so that numbers appear:

❖ With dollar signs, commas, or decimals

❖ Rounded off to a specific decimal place or a whole number

❖ Any combination of the above

You can also format numbers to appear as dates, times, or in a specialized format called *scientific notation*.

The entire worksheet can be set up in advance for a specific format or you can format numbers after you enter them. In this chapter you will:

❖ Format the numbers already in a worksheet

❖ Format non-adjacent cells with a single command

❖ Learn several ways to remove formats from a worksheet

INSERTING COMMAS IN NUMBERS

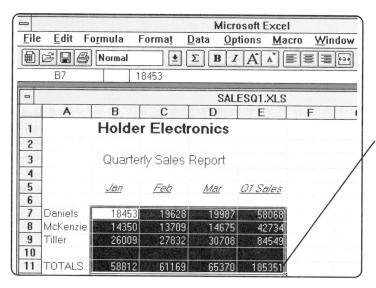

1. **Click** on **B7**. Leave the pointer in the cell.

2. **Press and hold** the mouse button and **drag** the pointer diagonally down to **E11**.

3. **Release** the mouse button when you have highlighted all of the numbers in B7 through E11.

4. Click on **Format** in the menu bar. A pull-down menu will appear.

5. Click on **Number**. The Number Format dialog box will appear.

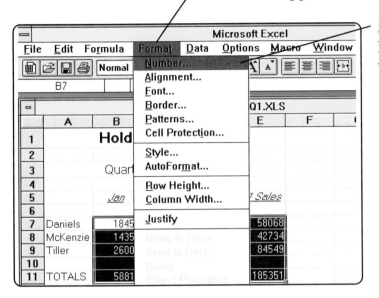

6. Click on **Number** in the Category list box.

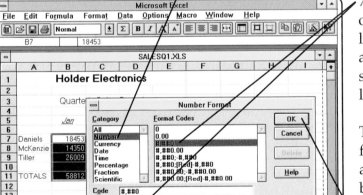

7. Click on **#,##0**, the third option in the Format Codes list box. Notice the Sample at the bottom of the box shows how a number will look in this particular format.

Try clicking on other formats to see how they affect the number. Then go back to the #,##0 format.

8. Click on **OK**. The numbers in the highlighted area will appear with commas. Any number entered outside the highlighted area will appear in the General format.

ADDING DOLLAR SIGNS

In this section you will add dollar signs to the numbers in the first and last rows. Excel has a special technique that allows you to select both rows and apply the command to both at the same time.

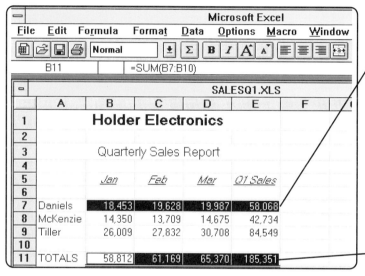

1. **Click** on **B7**. Leave the pointer in the cell.

2. **Press and hold** the mouse button and **drag** the pointer over to **E7**.

3. **Release** the mouse button when you have highlighted the range B7:E7. (B7:E7 is another way to say B7 to E7.)

4. **Press and hold** the **Ctrl** key and **repeat steps 1 through 3** to highlight B11 to F11. When you use the Ctrl key you can select non-adjacent cells or ranges.

5. **Click** on **Format** in the menu bar. A pull-down menu will appear.

6. **Click** on **Number**. The Number Format dialog box will appear.

7. Click on **Currency** in the Category list box.

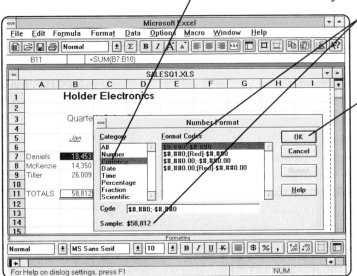

8. Click on the **first dollar sign option**. Notice the Sample shows how the number will look.

9. Click on **OK**.

If you had used this option when you formatted all of the numbers, they would all appear with dollar signs. By highlighting only the first and last rows, you applied the dollar sign format only to those rows.

REMOVING FORMATS FROM A WORKSHEET

If you decide you don't like a particular format, there are several ways to remove it.

Immediately After Applying It

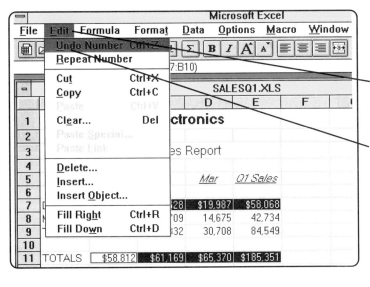

If you decide *right away* to remove a format, you can use the Edit menu.

1. Click on **Edit** in the menu bar. A pull-down menu will appear.

2. Click on **Undo Number**. The format will be removed. Note that Excel alters the Undo command to reflect your last step.

Removing a Format with the Toolbar

Many of the tools in the toolbar work like toggle switches. When you click on them a first time, you apply a specific format. When you click on them a second time, you remove the format.

1. **Highlight** the range **A1 to E3**. (See steps 1 to 3 in "Inserting Commas in Numbers," earlier in this chapter, if you need help.)

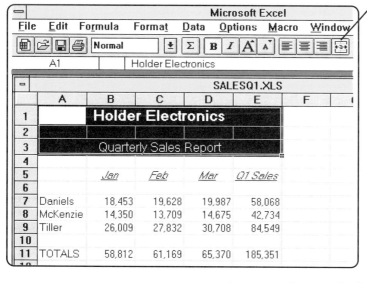

2. **Click** on the **Center Across Columns tool**. This will remove the centering and align both lines of text on the left of the highlighted area.

3. While the range is still highlighted, **click** again on the **Center Across Columns tool** to center the lines once more.

You can do this with the Bold tool, the Italics tool, and many other tools. Just for fun, try switching the italics in row 5 on and off a few times. You can make the words "dance." Experiment a little.

Removing a Format with a Shortcut Menu

You can remove the format in a cell at any time with a shortcut menu.

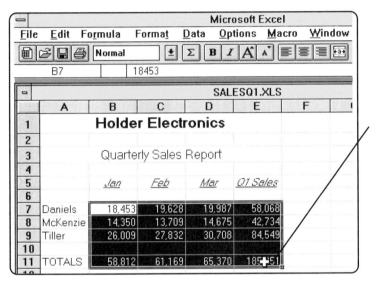

1. **Highlight** the range **B7 to E11**. (See steps 1 to 3 in "Inserting Commas in Numbers," earlier in this chapter, if you need help.)

2. **Leave** the pointer in cell E11.

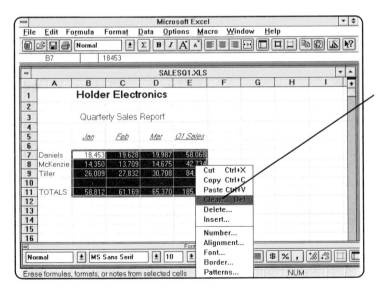

3. **Click** the **right mouse button**. A shortcut menu will appear.

4. **Click** on **Clear**. The Clear dialog box will appear.

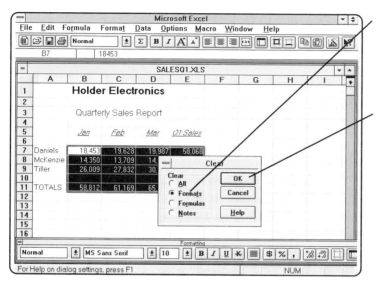

5. **Click** on **Formats** to leave the numbers and remove only the formatting.

6. **Click** on **OK**. The formatting will be removed from the highlighted cells.

Restoring the Deleted Formatting

1. **Click** on **Edit** in the menu bar. A pull-down menu will appear.

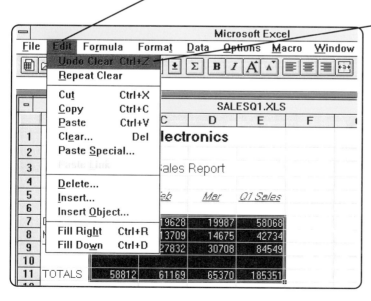

2. **Click** on **Undo Clear**. The formatting will be restored to the highlighted area. Notice that Excel altered the Undo command to reflect your last step.

If you want your worksheet to look like the examples in the rest of the book, go back to the section earlier in this chapter on "Adding Dollar Signs" and put the dollar signs back in rows 7 and 11.

CLOSING THE FORMATTING TOOLBAR

You can close the Formatting toolbar very easily.

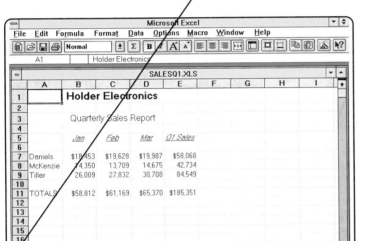

1. **Click** on the **Control menu box** (⊟) in the left corner of the Formatting toolbar. The toolbar will disappear from your screen. You can call it up again at any time and it will reappear in this same position.

If you cannot see the Control menu box on the toolbar, move the toolbar to the right. See steps 4 to 6 of "Changing the Position of a Toolbar" in Chapter 9 if you need help.

Program Manager

Part III: Multiple Worksheets and Formulas

Working with Multiple Worksheets

Opening a second worksheet is as easy as clicking on the New Worksheet tool in the toolbar. You can, of course, close one file before opening another. Or, you can keep two files on your screen at the same time so you can copy information from one worksheet into the other. In this chapter you will:

❖ Open a second worksheet

❖ Switch back and forth between two worksheets

❖ Arrange two worksheets so both are on your screen at the same time

❖ Copy data from one worksheet and paste it into a second worksheet

❖ Bring a worksheet to the foreground

OPENING A SECOND WORKSHEET

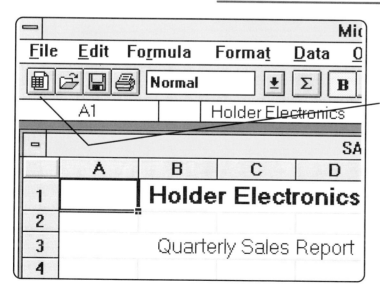

1. Open the **SALESQ1 worksheet** if it is not already on your screen.

2. Click on the **New Worksheet tool** in the toolbar. A worksheet entitled "Sheet2" will appear.

Notice that Sheet2 appears on top of SALESQ1. Sheet2 may even cover SALESQ1 completely. The bright-colored title bar tells you that Sheet2 is the *active worksheet*. The active worksheet (also called the *active window*) has a Control menu box (⊟) on the left of the title bar. It also has Minimize (▼) and Maximize (▲) buttons on the right of the title bar. The active worksheet is the one that will be affected by the next entry or command. If you can see the SALESQ1 worksheet, its dimmer title bar tells you this is the inactive worksheet. (The exact colors of the active and inactive title bars depend on the colors you set up in Windows. Refer to *Windows 3.1: The Visual Learning Guide* if you want to learn how to customize the colors on your screen.)

SWITCHING BETWEEN WORKSHEETS

In this section you will move back and forth between SALESQ1 and Sheet2.

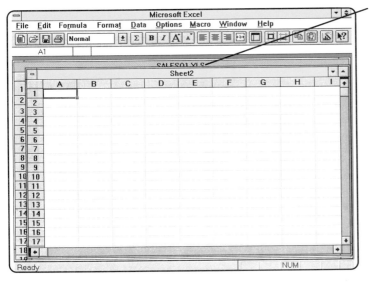

1. **Click** on any part of the **SALESQ1** worksheet you can see. The SALESQ1 worksheet becomes the active worksheet and comes to the foreground. Sheet2 becomes inactive and moves to the background.

If you cannot see SALESQ1, go on to the next section, "Arranging Worksheets so You Can See More Than One."

Now you will bring Sheet2 to the foreground again.

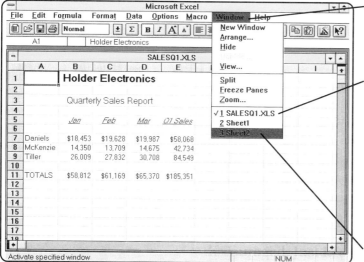

2. Click on **Window** in the menu bar. A pull-down menu will appear.

Notice the list of worksheets that have been opened. Sheet1 appeared when you opened Excel. Then you opened SALESQ1. Then you opened a new worksheet, which Excel labeled Sheet2.

3. Click on **Sheet2**. Sheet2 will come to the foreground.

ARRANGING WORKSHEETS SO YOU CAN SEE MORE THAN ONE

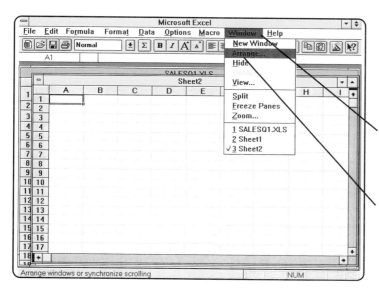

In this section you will arrange Sheet2 and SALESQ1 so that you can see both of them on your screen at the same time.

1. Click on **Window** in the menu bar. A pull-down menu will appear.

2. Click on **Arrange**. The Arrange Windows dialog box will appear.

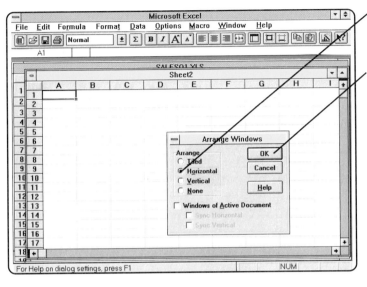

3. Click on **Horizontal** to put a black dot in the circle.

4. Click on **OK**. The dialog box will disappear and all the worksheets listed on the pull-down menu will appear layered horizontally on your screen.

Notice the three worksheets on your screen: Sheet2, SALESQ1, and Sheet1. Excel numbers the worksheets opened in any session in numerical order. Sheet1 appeared when you opened Excel. Therefore, the next blank worksheet you open is Sheet2. If you closed Sheet2 and opened another new worksheet, the new worksheet would be Sheet3. (The only way to stop the process is to exit Excel. When you open it again you will see Sheet1 on your screen.)

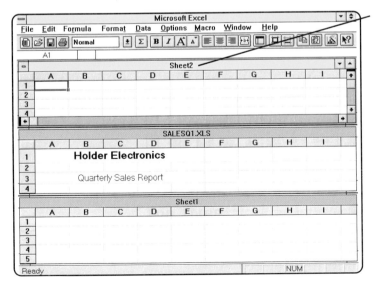

Sheet2 was the active worksheet when you chose the horizontal option, so it is the active window (or worksheet) in the horizontal display.

Since you will not be working with Sheet1, let's close it.

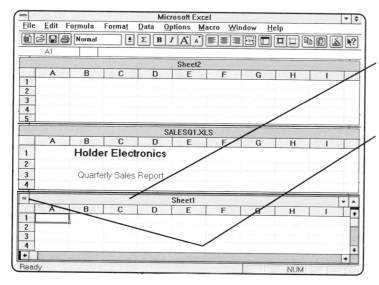

Closing Sheet1

1. **Click** on the **Sheet1 title bar** to make Sheet1 the active worksheet.

2. **Click twice** on the **Control menu box** (⊟) on the left of the Sheet1 title bar. Sheet1 will close.

Arranging the Remaining Worksheets

Now you have a space where Sheet1 was positioned. You can rearrange the remaining worksheets so they fill the space.

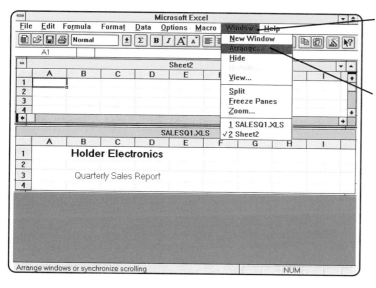

1. **Click** on **Window** in the menu bar. A pull-down menu will appear.

2. **Click** on **Arrange**. The Arrange Windows dialog box will appear.

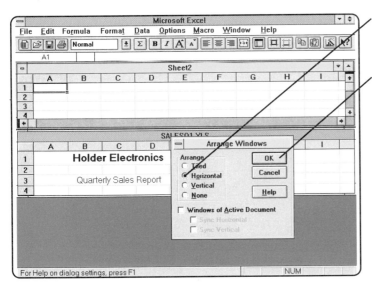

3. Confirm that **Horizontal** has a black dot in its circle.

4. Click on **OK**. Sheet2 and SALESQ1 will be enlarged to fill the entire space available.

Your screen will look like the example below.

COPYING BETWEEN WORKSHEETS

In this section, you will copy the heading and the salespeople's names from SALESQ1 to Sheet2.

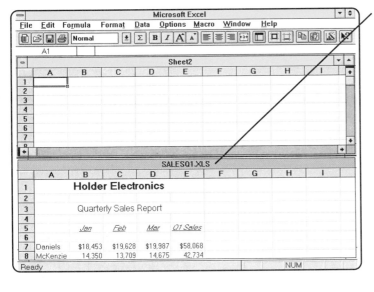

1. Click on the **SALESQ1** **title bar** to make SALESQ1 the active worksheet.

2. **Click** on **A1** on the SALESQ1 worksheet. Leave the cursor in the cell.

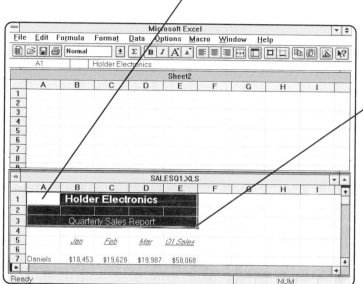

3. **Press and hold** the mouse button and **drag** the cursor to **E3**.

4. **Release** the mouse button when you have highlighted the range A1:E3. Keep the cursor in E3.

5. **Click** the **right mouse button**. A shortcut menu will appear.

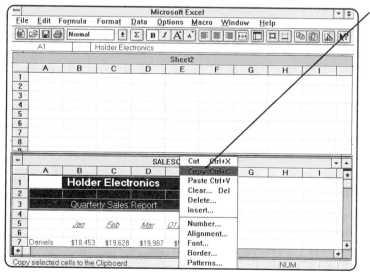

6. **Click** on **Copy**. The highlighted cells will be surrounded by a moving border. The cells are now copied to the Clipboard. The Clipboard is a storage area that holds copied, deleted, or cleared data. The fact that data goes to the Clipboard when it is deleted or cleared is the reason why you can undo the Delete or Clear command. The data will stay in the Clipboard until it is replaced with other data.

7. Click on the **Sheet2 title bar** to make it the active worksheet.

8. Click on **A1** in Sheet2. Leave the cursor in the cell.

9. Click the **right mouse button**. A shortcut menu will appear.

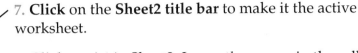

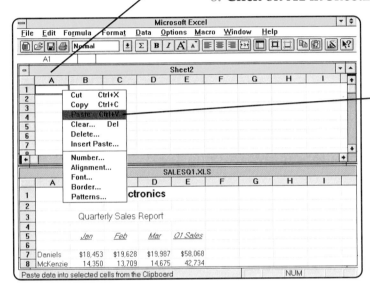

10. Click on **Paste**. The cells you copied from SALESQ1 to the Clipboard will be pasted into Sheet2 beginning at cell A1. The heading is not exactly right for this second worksheet, but you will change it in Chapter 12, "Formatting a Second Worksheet."

11. Click on the **SALESQ1 title bar** to make it the active worksheet. You will see the moving border around A1:E3.

12. Click on ↓ on the vertical scroll bar to bring the salespeople's names into view.

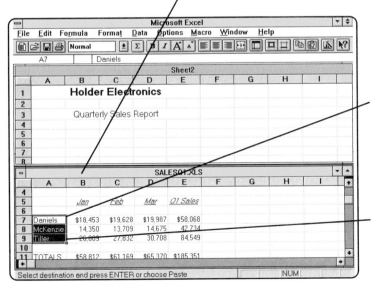

13. Click on **A7** in SALESQ1. Leave the cursor in the cell.

14. Press and hold the mouse button and **drag** the cursor down to **A9**.

15. Release the mouse button when you have highlighted the range A7:A9. Leave the cursor in A9.

16. Click the **right mouse button**. A shortcut menu will appear.

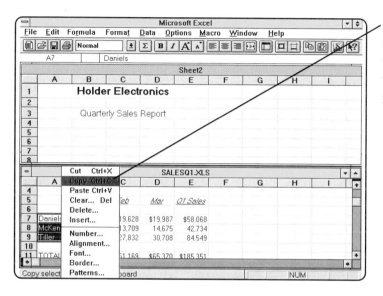

17. Click on **Copy**. The selected cells will be copied to the Clipboard. The cells will be surrounded by a moving border.

18. Click on the **Sheet2 title bar** to make it the active worksheet. The range A1:E3 will appear with the black highlight, indicating that it is still active.

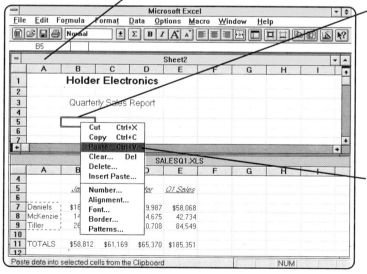

19. Click on cell **B5** on Sheet2. Leave the cursor in the cell. The black highlight will disappear from A1:E3.

20. Click the **right mouse button**. A shortcut menu will appear.

21. Click on **Paste**. The salespeople's names will be pasted into Sheet2 starting at cell B5.

BRINGING A WORKSHEET TO THE FOREGROUND

You won't be using SALESQ1 again for a while so you can arrange the worksheets so that Sheet2 is the only one you see.

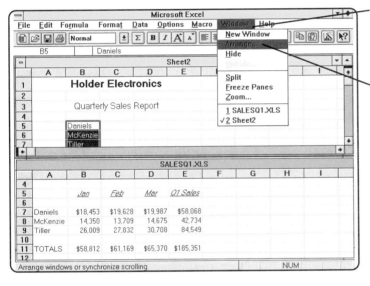

1. **Click** on **Window** in the menu bar. A pull-down menu will appear.

2. **Click** on **Arrange**. The Arrange Windows dialog box will appear.

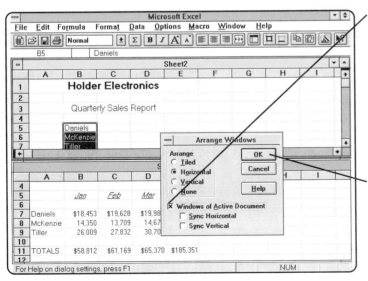

3. **Click** on **Windows of Active Document** to insert an X in the box. Since Sheet2 is the active document (or window), this option will enlarge Sheet2 to fill the available space.

4. **Click** on **OK**. Sheet2 will be enlarged and SALESQ1 will be hidden.

Formatting a Second Worksheet

In addition to the standard Windows functions of copying and pasting, Excel has a new feature, called drag and drop moving, that will come in handy as you format the second worksheet. In this chapter you will:

❖ Move data on a worksheet with drag and drop moving

❖ Pre-format the worksheet so that all numbers appear in a specific format

❖ Use the AutoFill feature to copy data to adjacent cells

DRAG AND DROP MOVING

If you followed the steps in Chapter 11, you copied the heading and the salespeople's names from SALESQ1 to Sheet2. If not, you will need to follow the steps in Chapter 11 before you do these procedures.

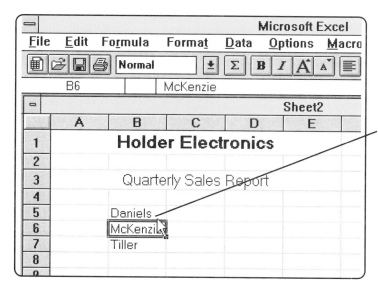

In this section you will move McKenzie and Tiller up to row 5.

1. **Click** on McKenzie in **B6**.

2. **Move** the pointer to the **border** of the cell. The pointer will change to an arrow. You may have to fiddle with the placement of the pointer to get it to change.

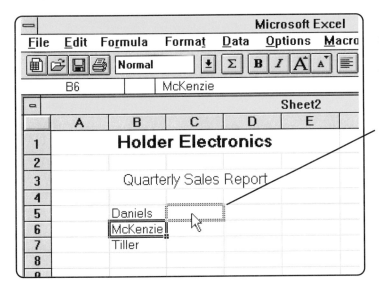

3. Press and hold the mouse button and **drag** the cell by its border up to **C5**. You will see an outline of the cell as you drag.

4. Release the mouse button when the outline is in C5. The contents of the cell will move to C5.

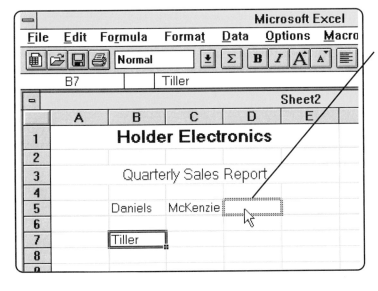

5. Click on Tiller in **B7**.

6. Repeat steps 2 and 3, but place the name in **D5**.

PRE-FORMATTING NUMBERS

In this section you will set up the worksheet for a specific number format. Any number entered into the worksheet will appear in that format.

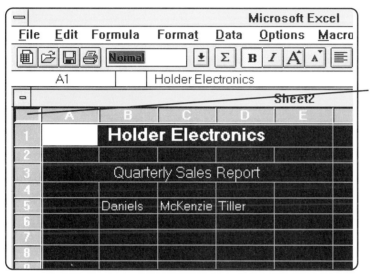

1. **Click** on the **Select All box** at the intersection of the row numbers and column headings. The entire worksheet will be highlighted in black (with the exception of the first cell in the range, which will remain white).

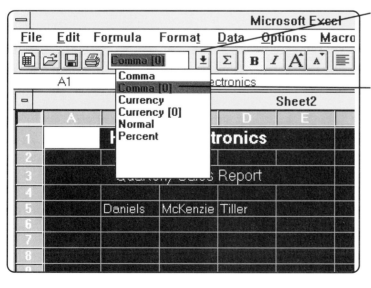

2. **Click** on ⬇ to the right of the Style box. A drop-down list will appear.

3. **Click** on **Comma [0]**. This will set up the worksheet so that any number entered into the worksheet will appear with commas and no decimal places (e.g. 25,000). Using the Style box is a formatting shortcut. You can also click on Format in the menu bar, then click on Style.

4. **Click** on **A1** to get rid of the highlighting.

EDITING COPIED DATA

In this section you will change the report name to "January Commission Report."

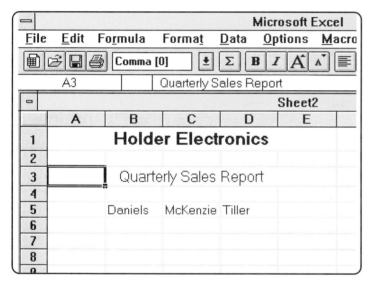

1. **Click** on **A3**. "Quarterly Sales Report" will appear in the formula bar. Now **click** on Quarterly **in B3**. Nothing appears in the formula bar. How strange! As far as Excel is concerned, "Quarterly Sales Report" is in A3 where you originally entered it. The fact that you centered it across columns affects only its appearance, not its original placement.

2. **Click** on **A3** again.

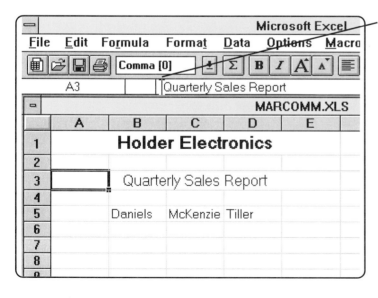

3. **Place** the pointer at the **beginning of Quarterly Sales Report** in the formula bar. The pointer will change to an I-beam.

4. **Press and hold** the mouse button and **drag** the I-beam over the words "Quarterly Sales." **Release** the mouse button when they are highlighted.

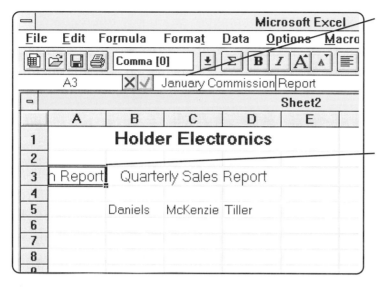

5. Type January Commission. Be sure there is a space after "Commission." January Commission will replace the highlighted words.

It's okay that the new words appear in A3 and Quarterly Sales Report is still on the worksheet. Quarterly Sales Report will disappear after step 6.

6. **Press Enter** or click on ✔ to enter the new words on the worksheet.

SAVING AND NAMING SHEET2

You have done quite a bit of work on this worksheet and you don't want to lose any of it.

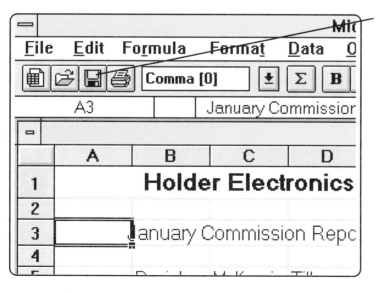

1. **Click** on the **Save File tool** in the toolbar. Since you have not yet named this file, the Save As dialog box will appear.

2. Since the File Name box is already highlighted, **type jancomm** (for January Commission). It will replace SHEET2.XLS as the worksheet title. Remember, a filename can have no more than eight characters. It doesn't matter if you type the filename in capital or small letters. It will appear in capital letters on the worksheet. Excel will automatically add the extension .XLS to identify it as a worksheet.

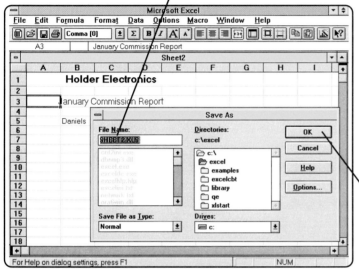

3. **Click** on **OK**. The dialog box will disappear and Sheet2 will appear with the new title JANCOMM.XLS.

INCREASING COLUMN WIDTH

You can increase column width with a menu command or with the mouse. Use a menu command when you want to increase a column to a specific width or when you want to increase the width of more than one column at the same time.

Using a Menu Command

In this section you will add the salespeople's first names to the worksheet. The longest name will have 15 characters. Therefore, you can increase the width of columns B, C, and D to 15 using a menu command.

1. **Click** on Daniels in **B5**. Leave the pointer in the cell.

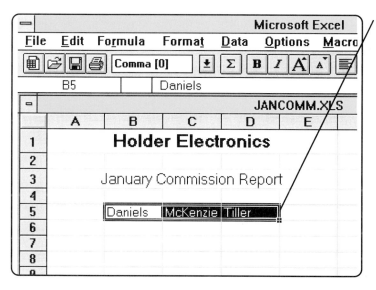

2. **Press and hold** the mouse button and **drag** the pointer over to Tiller in **D5**. The three names will be highlighted.

3. **Click** on **Format** in the menu bar. A pull-down menu will appear.

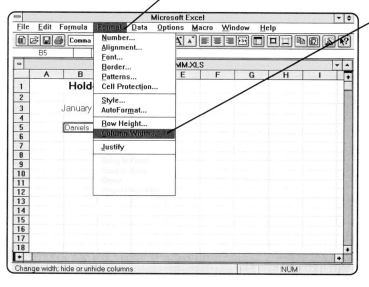

4. **Click** on **Column Width**. The Column Width dialog box will appear.

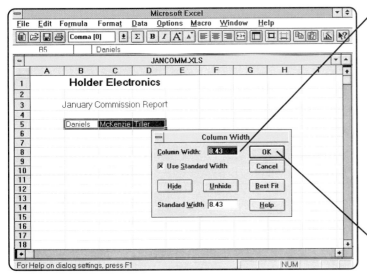

Notice that 8.43 in the Column Width box is highlighted. This is the standard column width in Excel. (Strange but true.)

5. Type 15 to increase the column width of the selected columns to 15. The 15 will replace the highlighted number 8.43.

6. Click on **OK**. Columns B, C, and D will be 15 characters wide.

Notice that the headings in rows 1 and 3 centered themselves over the wider columns.

7. **Click** on Daniels in **B5**.

8. **Place** the **cursor after Daniels** in the formula bar and **click** to set it in place.

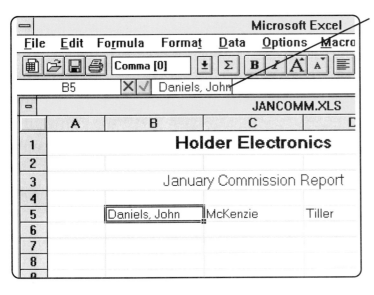

9. **Type** a **comma**, a **space**, and **John**. The name will become Daniels, John.

10. **Press Enter** to insert the edited name into the cell.

11. Repeat steps 7 through 10 to change McKenzie in C5 to **McKenzie, Susan**.

12. Repeat steps 7 through 10 to change Tiller in D5 to **Tiller, Stacey**.

13. Type Totals in E5. **Press Enter**.

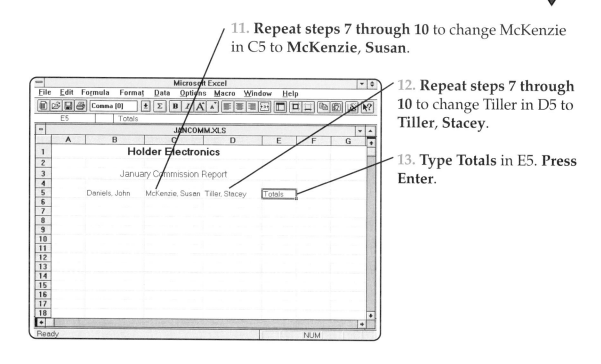

Using the Mouse

In this section you will use the mouse to increase the width of column A. When you use the mouse, Excel adjusts the column for the longest entry, called a *best fit* adjustment.

1. Click on **A7**.

2. Type Product A (@ $1.50).

3. Press Enter to insert the phrase in A7. Notice that the entry is too wide for the cell.

4. **Move** the mouse pointer up to the column headings. Place it on the **line between column A and column B**. It will change shape when you get it positioned correctly.

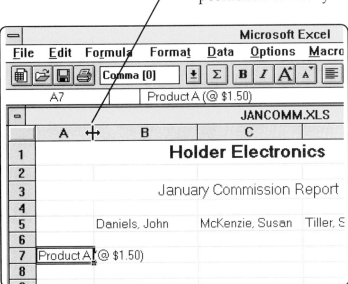

5. **Click twice** on the left mouse button. The column will increase to a best fit width.

Notice that the headings in rows 1 and 3 centered themselves again to accommodate the wider column A.

ENTERING ROW HEADINGS

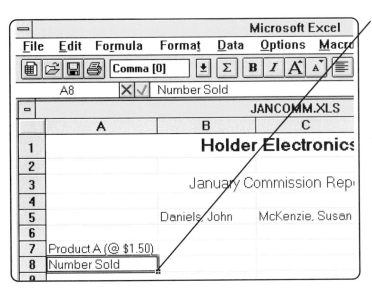

1. **Click on A8.** On your screen it will be empty.

2. **Type Number Sold.**

3. **Press Enter** or click on ✔ to insert the phrase into A8.

4. **Type** the **row headings** listed below in the appropriate cells. Remember that you can use the ↓ on your keyboard to enter data into a cell and automatically move down the column.

A9	Sales $
A11	Product B (@ $2.00)
A12*	Number Sold
A13*	Sales $
A15	Total Sales
A17	Commission (15%)

* You can use the Copy and Paste options on the shortcut menu to copy Number Sold and Sales $ from A8 and A9 to A12 and A13. (See steps 12 through 20 starting on page 80 if you need help.)

5. **Click** on ↓ on the vertical scroll bar to bring row 21 into view.

6. **Type** the **row headings** listed below in row 19 and row 21.

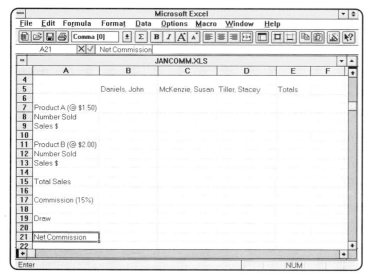

A19	Draw
A21	Net Commission

In the next section you will enter numbers into the worksheet. Then you will write formulas in Chapter 13, "Writing Formulas."

ENTERING NUMBERS

1. Type the **numbers** below in the appropriate cells. Since you pre-formatted the numbers to have commas, you don't have to type the commas. They will be inserted by Excel. (If you forget and type them, it won't do any harm.)

B8	C8	D8
3702	4784	5470

B12	C12	D12
6450	3587	8902

B19
1000

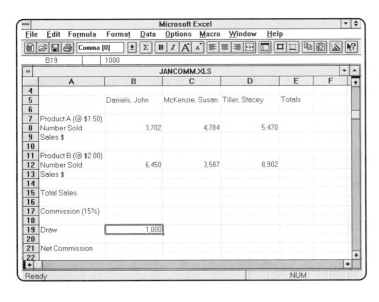

You will now use the AutoFill feature to copy the 1000 in B19 into C19 and D19.

USING AUTOFILL TO COPY

You used the AutoFill feature to complete a series of months in Chapter 1. You can also use AutoFill to copy the contents of a cell.

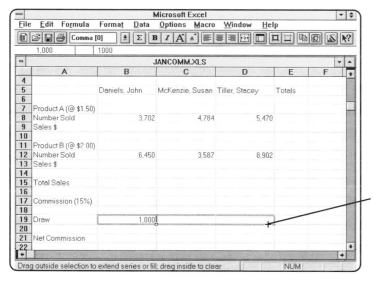

1. **Place** the pointer on the **fill handle** on cell **B19** (the small square in the lower-right corner of the cell border). The pointer will change to a black plus sign. You may have to fiddle with the placement to get it to change shape.

2. **Press and hold** the mouse button and **drag** the fill handle across to **D19**. The border of the cell will expand as you drag.

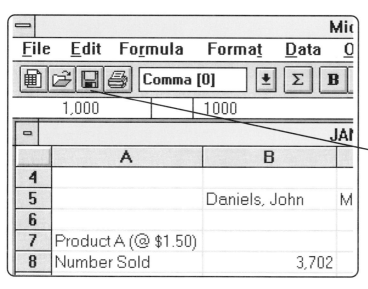

3. **Release** the mouse button when you have included B19:D19 in the border outline. The number in B19 (1,000) will be copied into C19 and D19.

4. **Click** on the **Save File tool** in the toolbar to save all your work.

Writing Formulas

Writing formulas is a breeze in Excel. You use standard symbols to designate mathematical processes. Addition is symbolized by a plus sign (+); subtraction by a hyphen (-); multiplication by an asterisk (*); and division by a forward slash (/).

In this chapter you will:

❖ Write formulas for addition, subtraction, multiplication, and percentage
❖ Add with the AutoSum tool
❖ Copy formulas to other cells

WRITING A MULTIPLICATION FORMULA

In this section you will write a formula to calculate Sales $ = Number Sold x Price.

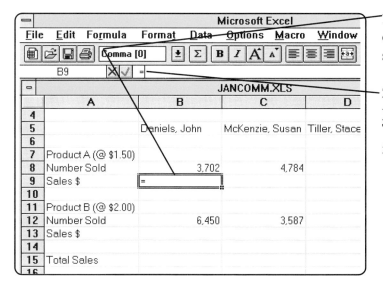

1. **Click** on **B9**, the Sales $ cell for Daniels. On your screen it will be empty.

2. **Type =** to tell Excel that you are starting a formula. The = will appear in the formula bar and in the cell.

97

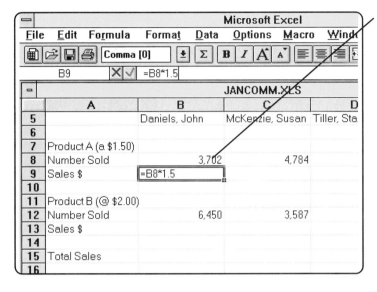

3. **Click** on 3,702 in **B8** to tell Excel that this is the first number in the formula. The cell reference (B8) will appear in the formula bar and in B9. A moving border will appear around B8.

4. **Type** * (the symbol for multiplication). The * will appear in the formula bar and in B9. The moving border will disappear from B8.

5. **Type 1.5** (for $1.50). The number will appear in the formula bar and in B9.

6. **Click** on ✔. The results of the multiplication formula (5,553) will appear in B9. The formula still appears in the formula bar.

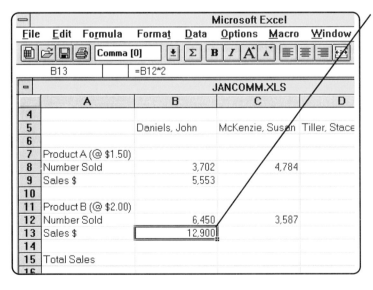

7. **Click** on **B13**. On your screen it will be empty.

8. **Repeat steps 2 through 6** to compute the Sales $ for Product B. Use 2 (for $2.00) as the price. You will see 12,900 in B13 when you finish.

WRITING AN ADDITION FORMULA

In this section you will write a formula to calculate Total Sales = Sales $ for Product A + Sales $ for Product B.

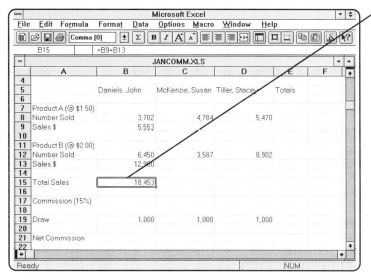

1. **Click** on **B15**, the Total Sales cell for Daniels. On your screen it will be blank.

2. **Type** = to indicate the start of a formula. The = will appear in the cell and in the formula bar.

3. **Click** on 5,553 in **B9**. The cell reference will appear in the formula bar and in B15. A moving border will appear around B9.

4. **Type** + to indicate addition. The + will appear in the formula bar and in B15. The moving border will disappear from B9.

5. **Click** on 12,900 in **B13**. The cell reference will appear in the formula bar and in B15. A moving border will appear around B13.

6. **Click** on ✔. Excel will make the calculations and enter the result of the formula (18,453) into B15.

WRITING A FORMULA TO CALCULATE A PERCENT

In this section you will write a formula to calculate Commission = Total Sales x 15 percent.

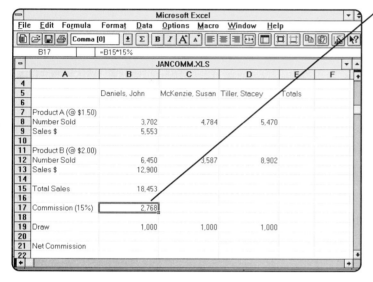

1. **Click** on **B17**, the Commission cell for Daniels. On your screen it will be blank.

2. **Type** = to tell Excel that you are writing a formula.

3. **Click** on 18,453 in **B15**. A moving border will appear around the cell. The cell reference will appear in the formula bar and in B17.

4. **Type** * to indicate multiplication. The * will appear in the formula bar and in B17.

5. **Type 15%** to multiply 18,453 by 15 percent. It will appear in the formula bar and in B17.

6. **Click** on ✔ or press Enter. Excel will make the calculations and enter the result (2,768) into B17. Fifteen percent of 18,453 is actually 2,767.95. Since you selected a number format with no decimal places, the number will be rounded to the nearest whole number.

WRITING A SUBTRACTION FORMULA

In this section you will write a formula to calculate
Net Commission = Commission - Draw.

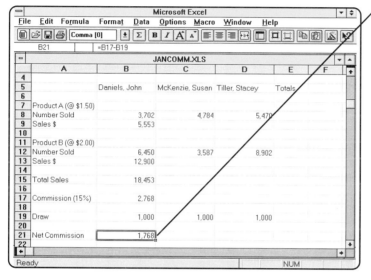

1. **Click** on **B21**. On your screen it will be empty.

2. **Type** = to start a formula. The = will appear in the formula bar and in B21.

3. **Click** on **B17**. A moving border will appear around the cell. The cell reference (B17) will appear in the formula bar and in B21.

4. **Type** - to indicate subtraction. The moving border around B17 will disappear.

5. **Click** on **B19**. A moving border will appear around the cell. The cell reference will be added to the formula bar and to B21.

6. **Click** on ✔. Excel will make the calculations and enter the result (1,768) into B21.

ADDING WITH THE AUTOSUM TOOL

In this section you will use the AutoSum tool in the toolbar to add the figures in rows 8, 12, and 19.

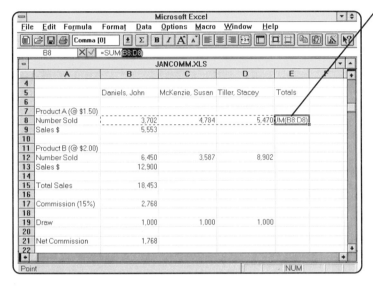

1. **Click** on **E8**. On your screen it will be empty.

2. **Click** on the **AutoSum tool** (Σ) in the toolbar. The formula to add the figures in row 8 [SUM(B8:D8)] will appear in the formula bar and in E8. The row will be surrounded by a moving border.

3. **Click** on ✔. Excel will make the calculations and enter the result (13,956) into E8.

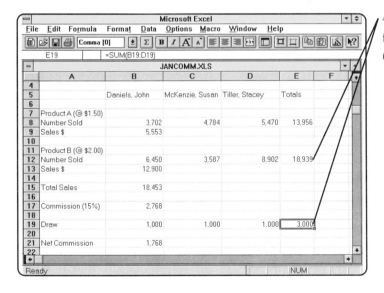

4. **Repeat steps 1 through 3** to enter the totals into E12 (18,939) and E19 (3,000).

COPYING FORMULAS

Now that all your formulas are written, you can copy them to other cells.

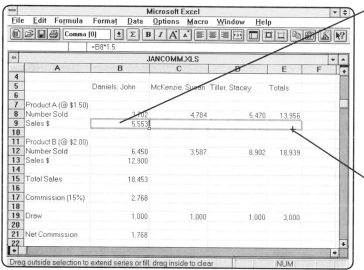

1. **Click** on **B9**.

2. **Place** the mouse pointer on the **fill handle** (the small square in the lower-right corner of the cell border). The pointer will change to a black plus sign.

3. **Press and hold** the mouse button and **drag** the fill handle across to **E9**. The border of the cell will expand as you drag.

4. **Release** the mouse button when you have included B9:E9 in the border outline. The formula contained in B9 will be copied across the rows and the totals will appear in the highlighted cells.

5. **Repeat steps 1 to 4** to copy the formulas in rows 13, 15, 17, and 21. Your worksheet will look like the example to the left.

Using AutoFormat

AutoFormat is another of Excel's special features. It contains a selection of pre-designed formats that you can apply to your worksheets. You can even customize the pre-designed formats. In this chapter you will:

❖ Use the AutoFormat feature, choosing from the selection of pre-designed formats

❖ Customize the AutoFormat

❖ Remove an AutoFormat design

SELECTING A FORMAT WITH AUTOFORMAT

In this section you will choose a format from the selection of pre-designed formats and apply it to your worksheet.

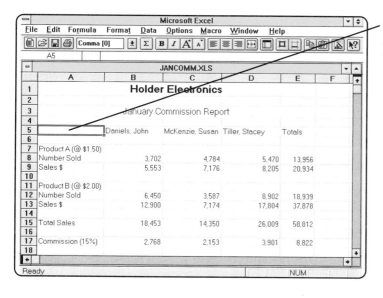

1. **Click** on **A5**. Leave the pointer in the cell.

2. **Press and hold** the mouse button and **drag** the pointer down and across to **E21**. The worksheet will automatically scroll up to show more rows as you drag the cursor down and across the worksheet. **Release** the mouse button when all of the numbers in your worksheet are included in the highlighting.

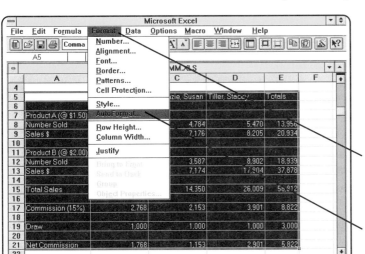

3. **Click** on **Format** in the menu bar. A pull-down menu will appear.

4. **Click** on **AutoFormat**. The AutoFormat dialog box will appear.

The AutoFormat dialog box contains a list of 14 pre-designed worksheet formats. As you click on a choice in the Table Format list box, the Sample box will show what that choice looks like. Browse through the list to see what your choices are.

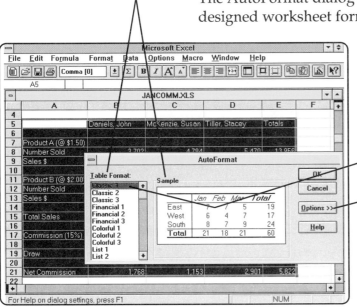

5. **Click** on **Classic 1**.

6. **Click** on **Options**. The AutoFormat dialog box will expand at the bottom to show the format options you can apply.

CUSTOMIZING AUTOFORMAT DESIGNS

AutoFormat designs have specific number formats, font selections, data alignment formats, border styles, background patterns, and column and row width/height choices. You can customize any of these by applying your own choice of format and turning off the format that comes with the pre-designed selection.

In "Pre-Formatting Numbers" in Chapter 12 you applied a specific number format to the worksheet. Since you don't want to override this format, turn off the number format of this AutoFormat selection.

1. Click on **Number** to *remove* the ✕ from the box. The Classic 1 format will be applied to your worksheet and the number format you chose in Chapter 12 will remain in effect.

Notice that these automatic formats do not include titles and subtitles. This is why you did not include "Holder Electronics" and "March Commission Report" in the highlighting.

2. Click on **OK**. The Classic 1 format (minus the number format) will be applied to your worksheet.

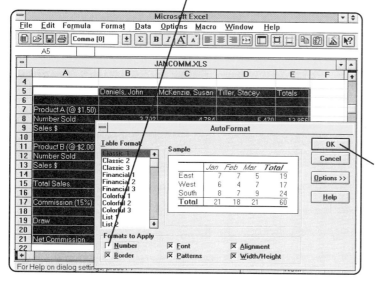

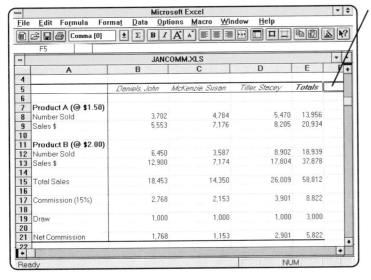

3. Click anywhere off the highlighted area to get rid of the highlighting.

Notice the formatting that has been applied to the worksheet.

REMOVING AN AUTOFORMAT DESIGN

If you decide you don't like a format that was just applied, you can remove it with the Edit option in the menu bar.

1. Click on **Edit** in the menu bar. A pull-down menu will appear.

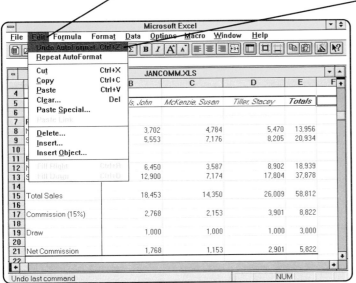

2. Click on **Undo AutoFormat**. (Notice that Excel kept track of your last move and changed the Undo command to reflect it.)

3. If you want to replace the format, **click** on **Edit** again. Then **click** on **Redo AutoFormat**.

You can remove a format at any time with a shortcut menu. See Chapter 10, "Removing a Format with a Shortcut Menu."

Working with Large Worksheets

When you work with a large worksheet it is annoying to watch the column and row headings scroll out of sight. Excel solves this problem by letting you freeze parts of your worksheet into separate sections, or *panes*, which always remain in view. It also lets you change the view so more of the worksheet is visible on your screen. In this chapter you will:

❖ Freeze and unfreeze a row and column (panes)

❖ Change the view (zoom out) so you can see more of the worksheet on your screen

❖ Close all opened worksheets

FREEZING ROWS AND COLUMNS

In this section you will freeze the screen so that row 5 and column A are always visible. You should have JANCOMM.XLS on your screen.

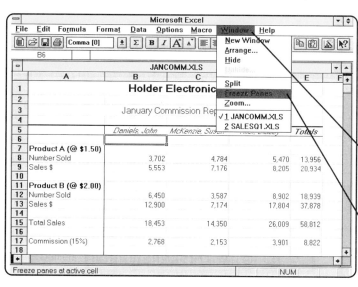

1. Click on **B6**. This will be the "freezing point."

2. Click on **Window** in the menu bar. A pull-down menu will appear.

3. Click on **Freeze Panes**. Your screen will be frozen above and to the left of B6.

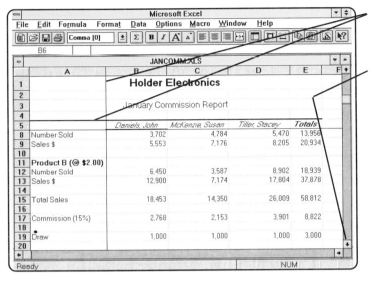

Notice the freeze lines on the worksheet.

4. Click twice on ↓ on the vertical scroll bar to move down the worksheet. Notice that row 5 remains in view even though rows 6 and 7 have scrolled out of sight.

5. Click twice on ➡ on the horizontal scroll bar to move to the right on the worksheet. Notice that column A remains in view even though columns B and C have scrolled out of sight.

Going Home

Normally when you press Ctrl + Home you return to A1. When you have frozen your worksheet, you will return to the "freezing point," which in this example is B6.

1. Press and hold the **Ctrl** key. Then **press** the **Home** key (Ctrl + Home). You will return to B6.

UNFREEZING PANES

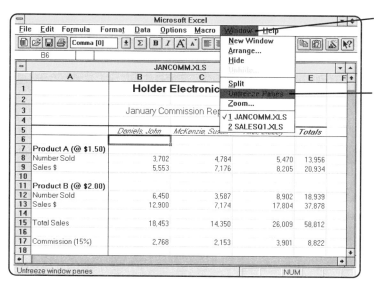

1. Click on **Window** in the menu bar. A pull-down menu will appear.

2. Click on **Unfreeze Panes**.

It doesn't matter where the cursor is when you unfreeze panes.

CHANGING THE SCREEN VIEW

The Zoom feature in Excel is like the zoom lens on a camera. You can *zoom out* and fit more of the worksheet on the screen. Or, you can *zoom in* and magnify a specific area.

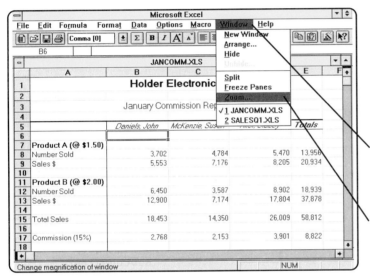

Zooming Out

In this section you will zoom out so that more of the worksheet is visible on your screen.

1. **Click** on **Window** in the menu bar. A pull-down menu will appear.

2. **Click** on **Zoom**. The Zoom dialog box will appear.

3. **Click** on **75%** to reduce the worksheet to 75% of its original size.

4. **Click** on **OK**.

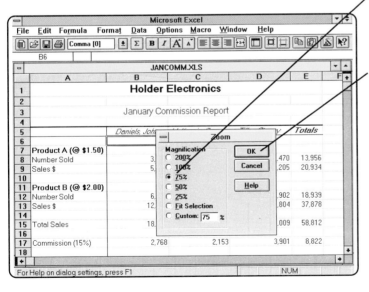

The worksheet will be reduced in size on your screen, making more columns and rows visible. This affects the screen view only. It does not affect the printed version of your worksheet.

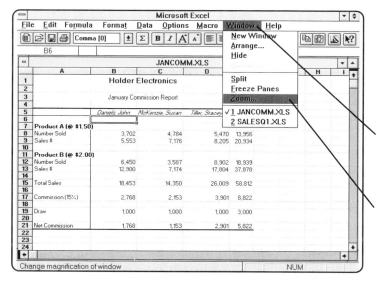

Zooming In

In this section you will return to the standard (100%) view.

1. **Click** on **Window** in the menu bar. A pull-down menu will appear.

2. **Click** on **Zoom**. The Zoom dialog box will appear.

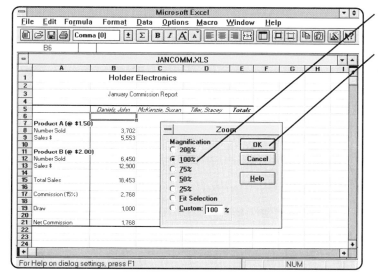

3. **Click** on **100%**.

4. **Click** on **OK**. The worksheet will be restored to standard (100%) size.

CLOSING ALL WORKSHEETS

In preparation for the next chapter, "Linking Two Worksheets," you will close SALESQ1.XLS and JANCOMM.XLS. There is a special command to close all open worksheets. If you have only one worksheet open, the steps will still work.

1. Press and hold the **Shift** key and **click** on **File** in the menu bar. A pull-down menu will appear.

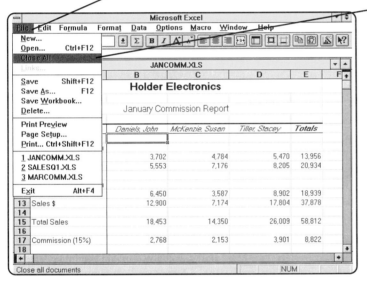

2. Click on **Close All**. (The Close command changed to Close All when you held down the Shift key.)

If you made any changes in the worksheets without saving them, you will see a dialog box asking if you want to save changes. Click on Yes to save. If there were no changes to be saved, the worksheets will simply close and you will be returned to an empty Excel screen.

Linking Two Worksheets

When you establish a *link* between two worksheets, any change made in the linked data on the first worksheet (the *source* worksheet) is immediately reflected in the linked data on the second worksheet (the *dependent* worksheet). The process of creating links is very easy. In this chapter you will:

❖ Open JANCOMM.XLS as the source worksheet and a new worksheet as the dependent worksheet

❖ Arrange both worksheets horizontally on your screen

❖ Link the worksheets

❖ Test the link

❖ Save both worksheets

GETTING READY TO LINK

In this section you will open JANCOMM.XLS. This will be the *source* worksheet, since it contains the commission data that will be transferred to a second worksheet. Then you will open a new worksheet that will become the *dependent* worksheet and receive the data from the source worksheet.

Complete the steps in the section "Closing All Worksheets" in Chapter 15 if you haven't done so already. Your screen should look like this example.

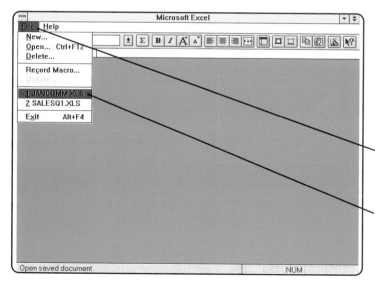

Opening the Worksheets

1. **Click** on **File** in the menu bar. A pull-down menu will appear.

2. **Click** on **JANCOMM.XLS.** It will appear on your screen.

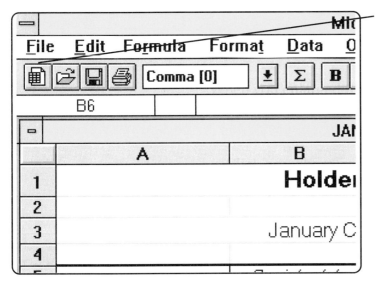

3. **Click** on the **New Worksheet tool** in the toolbar. A new worksheet will appear on your screen. If you have been following along with these procedures it will be Sheet3. It's okay if it has a different number.

Entering Data in the New Worksheet

1. **Click** on **A1**. On your screen it will be empty.

2. **Type Name**.

3. **Press Enter** to insert "Name" into A1.

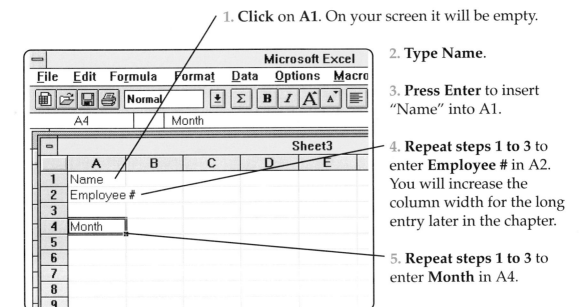

4. **Repeat steps 1 to 3** to enter **Employee #** in A2. You will increase the column width for the long entry later in the chapter.

5. **Repeat steps 1 to 3** to enter **Month** in A4.

Entering a Series of Months

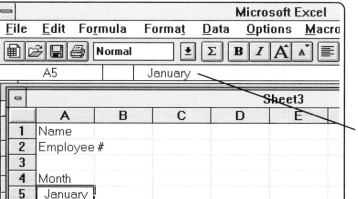

In this section you will enter a series of months in column A.

1. **Click** on **A5**. On your screen it will be empty.

2. **Press** the **spacebar** on your keyboard **twice**, then **type January**. This will indent January two spaces.

3. **Place** the pointer on the **fill handle** (the small square in the lower-right corner of the cell border). It will change to a black plus sign. You may have to fiddle with the placement to get the pointer to change shape.

4. **Press and hold** the mouse button as you **drag** the fill handle down to **A16**. The bottom border of the cell will expand as you drag.

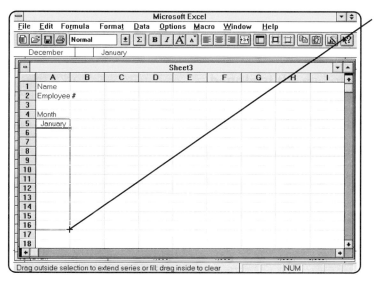

5. **Release** the mouse button when you have included A5:A16 in the border outline. The series January through December will appear in the cells. If you dragged too far down column A and the series started to repeat itself, simply drag the fill handle up to remove the extra months. Notice that the entire series is indented two spaces.

Increasing Cell Width

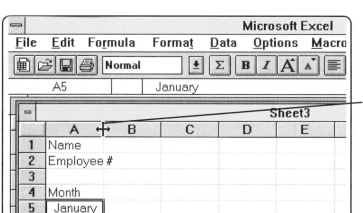

In this section you will use the mouse to increase the width of column A to make room for the longest entry.

1. **Move** the pointer up to the column headings and place it on the **line between columns A and B**. It will change shape.

2. **Click twice** on the mouse button. The column will expand to a *best fit* width.

Entering a Number as Text

In this section you will enter the employee number for Tiller. Since this is for identification purposes only, you don't want Excel to treat it as an actual number. If you type an apostrophe before the number, Excel will treat it as text. The number will appear aligned on the left in the cell like any other text.

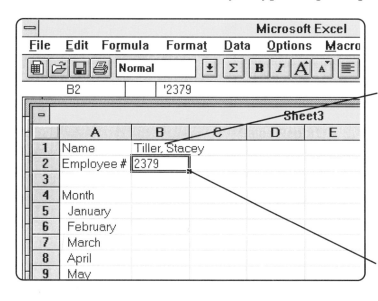

1. **Click** on **B1**. On your screen it will be empty. **Type Tiller, Stacey** and **press ↓** on your keyboard to enter the name in the cell and move to B2.

2. **Type '2379**. Don't forget the apostrophe.

3. **Press Enter** to insert the number into B2.

Formatting the Worksheet

In this section you will format the worksheet to have commas and two decimal places.

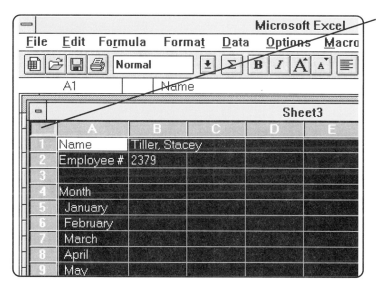

1. **Click** on the **Select All box** at the intersection of the row and column headings. The entire worksheet will be highlighted.

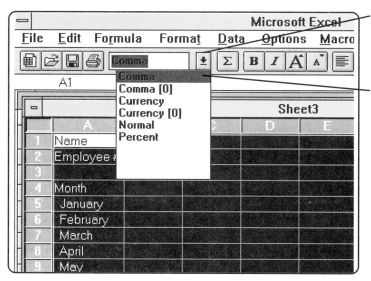

2. **Click** on ↓ to the right of the Style box. A drop-down list will appear.

3. **Click** on **Comma**. Any number with four or more digits entered into the worksheet will now appear with commas and all numbers will have decimal places (e.g., 2,500.00).

4. **Click anywhere** on the **worksheet** to get rid of the highlighting.

Now that Sheet3 is formatted, you are ready to link it to JANCOMM.XLS.

MAKING THE LINK

The easiest way to begin linking two worksheets is to first arrange them on your screen so you can move back and forth between them.

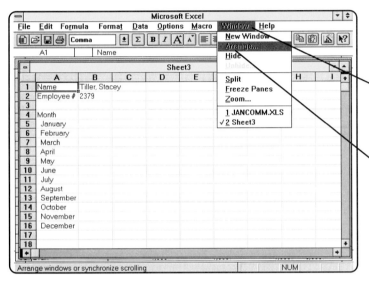

Arranging the Worksheets

1. Click on **Window** in the menu bar. A pull-down menu will appear.

2. Click on **Arrange**. The Arrange Windows dialog box will appear.

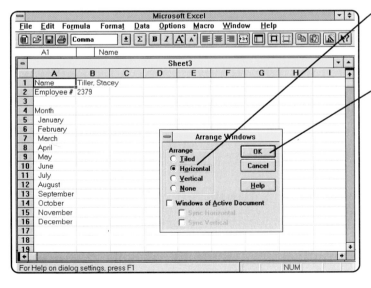

3. Click on **Horizontal** to insert a black dot in the circle.

4. Click on **OK**. JANCOMM.XLS and Sheet3 will be arranged horizontally on your screen. In Windows terminology, this is called *tiling*. (You can also tile vertically. In the vertical setup the files are arranged side by side on the screen.)

Copying Data to the Clipboard

In this section you will copy the commission data from cell D17 of JANCOMM.XLS to the Clipboard.

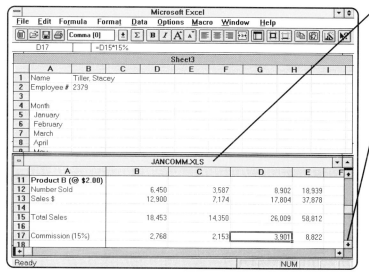

1. **Click anywhere** on **JANCOMM.XLS** to make it the active window. This will put scroll bars into the worksheet so you can move around in it.

2. **Click repeatedly** on ⬇ on the scroll bar to bring row 17 into view.

3. **Click** on 3,901 in **D17**. Leave the pointer in the cell.

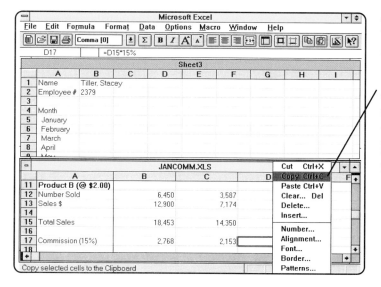

4. **Click** the **right mouse button**. A shortcut menu will appear.

5. **Click** on **Copy**. The cell contents will be copied to the Clipboard. The cell will be surrounded with a moving border.

6. **Click** on the **Sheet3 title bar** to make it the active worksheet.

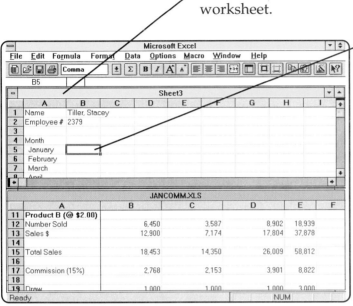

7. **Click** on **B5**. This is the cell into which you will paste-link the commission data you copied from JANCOMM.XLS.

Paste-Linking the Data into the Second Worksheet

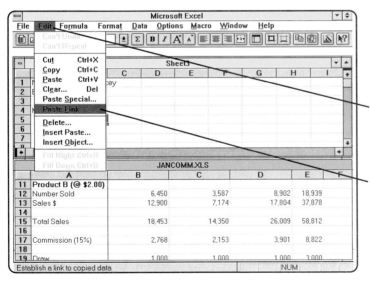

In this section you will paste-link the data from JANCOMM.XLS into the new worksheet.

1. **Click** on **Edit** in the menu bar. A pull-down menu will appear.

2. **Click** on **Paste Link**. The number that you copied to the Clipboard from JANCOMM.XLS will appear in B5 on Sheet3.

Notice that the number appears with two decimal places even though it had no decimal places on the source worksheet. That is because the number format you assigned to this worksheet included commas and decimal places. When the format of the source and dependent worksheets are different, it is the format of the dependent worksheet that controls the appearance of the data in the dependent worksheet.

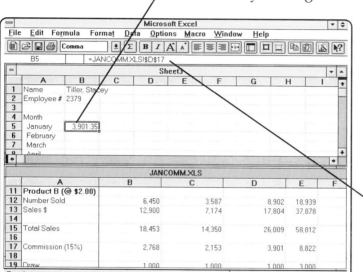

The "=JANCOMM.XLS" in the formula bar shows that this cell is the result of a formula on the JANCOMM.XLS worksheet. The "!" means that it is linked. The dollar signs ("$D$17") indicate that Excel will always look in this specific cell in the source worksheet for the data to link to the dependent worksheet.

In the next section you will have a little fun and test the link. You can do this by changing the commission amount of JANCOMM.XLS and then watching the change reflected in the linked data on Sheet3. However, you cannot simply change the commission amount because it is the result of a formula. You must change the numbers that are part of the formula. The formula for the commission amount was Total Sales x 15%. Since Total Sales itself is the result of a formula, you must change one of the numbers in the Total Sales formula to change the Total Sales amount and ultimately the commission amount. It gets complicated, doesn't it?

TESTING THE LINK

In this section you will make a change in the data in the source worksheet and watch as it affects the data in the dependent worksheet.

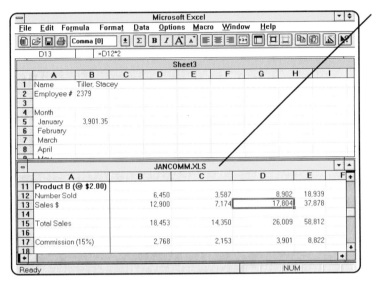

1. **Click** on the **title bar** of the JANCOMM.XLS worksheet to make it the active worksheet.

2. **Click** on 17,804 in **D13**.

3. **Type 30000** and **press Enter** to insert the new number into D13.

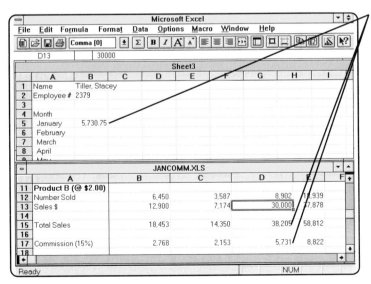

Notice that Total Sales in D15 on JANCOMM.XLS becomes 38,205. The Commission amount in D17 becomes 5,731. And the amount in B5 on Sheet3 becomes 5,730.75.

Undoing the Change

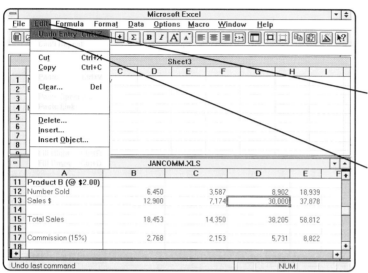

You can undo the change very easily (as long as you do it immediately).

1. **Click** on **Edit** in the menu bar. A pull-down menu will appear.

2. **Click** on **Undo Entry**. The original numbers will be restored.

SAVING LINKED WORKSHEETS

Always save a source worksheet before saving the dependent worksheet. This ensures that the links remain up to date.

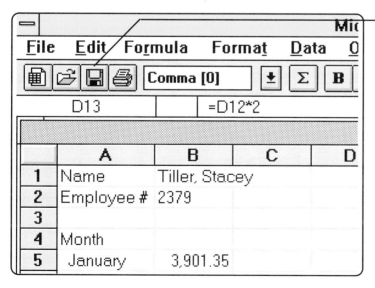

1. Since JANCOMM.XLS is the active worksheet, **click** on the **Save File tool** in the toolbar. JANCOMM.XLS will be saved.

2. **Click** on the **title bar** in Sheet3 to make Sheet3 the active window.

3. **Click** on the **Save File tool** in the toolbar. Since you have not named this file yet, the Save As dialog box will appear.

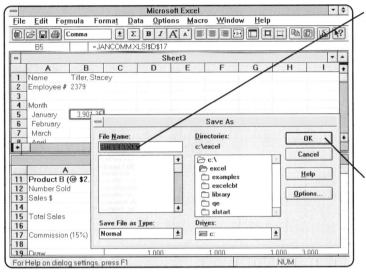

4. The File Name text box is already highlighted, so **type tiller**. It will replace the highlighted Sheet3.XLS already there. Excel will automatically add the .XLS extension when you close the dialog box.

5. Click on **OK**.

6. Press and hold the **Shift** key and **click** on **File** in the menu bar. A pull-down menu will appear.

7. Click on **Close All**.

The worksheets will close and you will see an empty Excel screen.

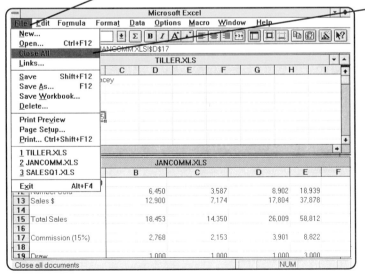

Program Manager

Part IV: Charts

Creating and Saving a Column Chart

With Excel's ChartWizard tool, you can create a chart (a graphic representation of your worksheet) automatically. You can choose from 14 types of charts. You can also select from a number of pre-designed formats. In this chapter, you will:

❖ Create a simple column chart using the ChartWizard

❖ Add a chart title and legend

❖ Add category and value titles

❖ Save the chart

USING THE CHARTWIZARD

Before you can create a chart, you must select the text and numbers you want to include in the chart.

Selecting the Chart Text

1. **Open** the **SALESQ1 worksheet** you created in Parts I and II. Refer to Chapter 7, "Opening a Saved File," if you need help.

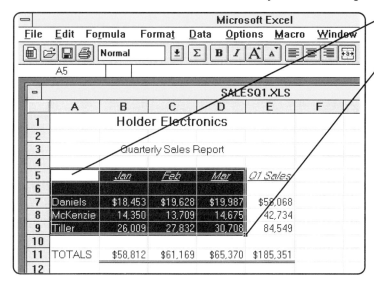

2. **Move** the mouse pointer to **A5**.

3. **Press and hold** the mouse button as you **drag** the pointer diagonally down to **D9**. **Release** the mouse button when you have highlighted the salespeople's names and the sales data for Jan, Feb, and Mar (cells A5 to D9). Do not highlight the totals in column E and row 11.

129

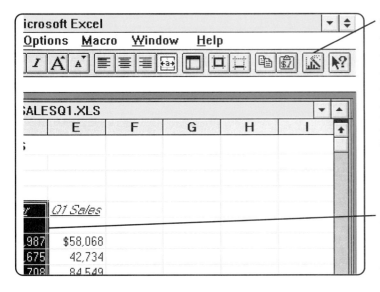

4. **Click** on the **ChartWizard tool**. It should be the second tool from the right on your toolbar. If you are using Excel at work or someone has used Excel on your computer before you, it's possible that the ChartWizard tool is in another location on the toolbar.

Notice that the cells you highlighted in step 3 are surrounded by a moving border.

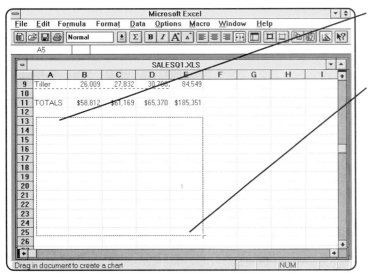

5. **Move** the mouse pointer to **A13**. The pointer will be a black plus sign.

6. **Press and hold** the mouse button as you **drag** the pointer diagonally down to **E25**. (This process tells Excel where to place your chart when it is created.) Don't be concerned that you cannot see row 25 right now. As you drag the cursor down, the screen will automatically show more rows. When cells A13 to E25 have been highlighted, **release** the mouse button. The ChartWizard – Step 1 of 5 dialog box will appear. The dialog box may appear in a different location than you see in the next example.

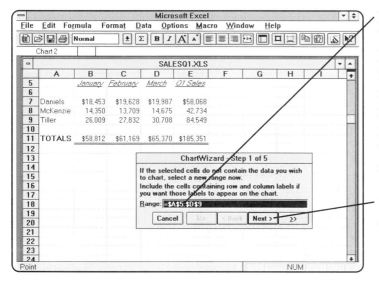

Notice that the Range text box refers to the cells you highlighted in step 3. If this is not correct, you can type in the correct cell reference now. The correct cell range is $A$5:$D$9. This means you have highlighted the range of cells A5 to D9.

7. **Click** on **Next**. The ChartWizard – Step 2 of 5 dialog box will appear.

Selecting a Column Chart

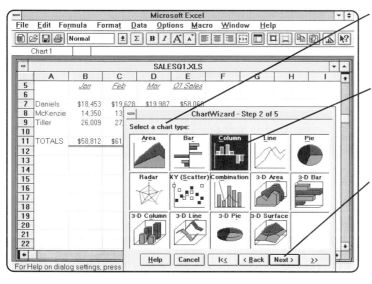

Notice the 14 different charts you can create with this dialog box.

1. **Click** on the **Column chart tool** if it is not already highlighted. If it is highlighted, go on to step 2.

2. **Click** on **Next**. The ChartWizard – Step 3 of 5 dialog box will appear.

Selecting the Chart Format

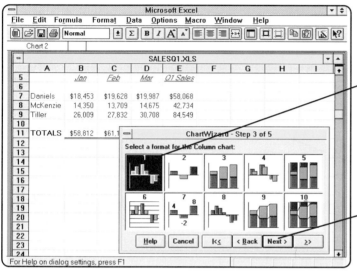

Notice the 10 different column chart formats you can create with this dialog box.

1. Click on the **Standard Column chart icon** (selection number 1) if it is not already highlighted. If it is highlighted, go on to step 2.

2. Click on **Next**. The ChartWizard – Step 4 of 5 dialog box will appear.

Previewing Your Chart

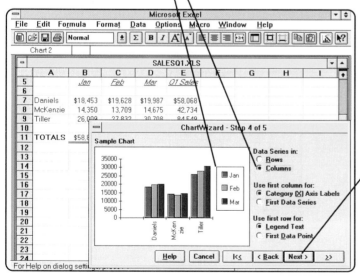

1. If your chart legend box does not show Jan, Feb, and Mar in the Preview screen, **click** on **Columns** to place a black dot in the center of the circle. After you click on Columns, the Rows circle will no longer be selected and Jan, Feb, and Mar will now show in the legend box. If they don't, **click** on **Cancel** and go back to the beginning of the chapter to make sure you highlighted the correct cells (A5 to D9).

2. Click on **Next**. The ChartWizard – Step 5 of 5 dialog box will appear.

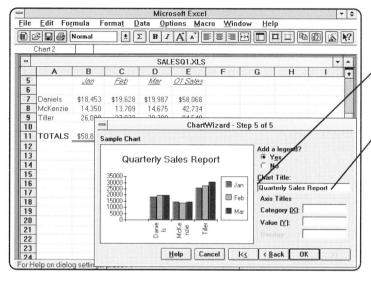

Adding a Chart Title

1. **Click** on the **Chart Title text box** to set the cursor in the box.

2. **Type Quarterly Sales Report**. *Do not press Enter or click on OK* until you have completed steps 1 to 5 in the following section. Notice that "Quarterly Sales Report" appears almost immediately in the Preview screen.

Adding Category and Value Titles

In Excel X and Y axes titles are called *Category titles* (X axis) and *Value titles* (Y axis). You will add the label "Top Three" to the X axis where the names of the salespeople appear and "Dollars" to explain that the numbers on the Y axis scale represent money.

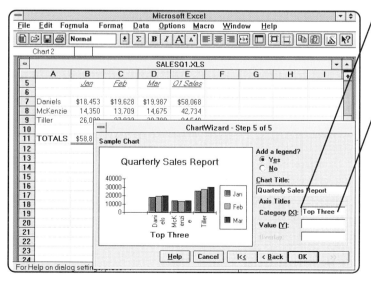

1. **Click** on the **Category [X] text box** to set the cursor in the box. On your screen the text box will be empty.

2. **Type Top Three**. *Do not press Enter or click on OK.* Notice that "Top Three" appears almost immediately in the preview screen. Excel automatically renumbers and shortens the dollar scale (Y axis) to make room for "Top Three."

3. **Click** on the **Value [Y] text box** to set the cursor in the box. On your screen the text box will be empty.

4. **Type Dollars**.

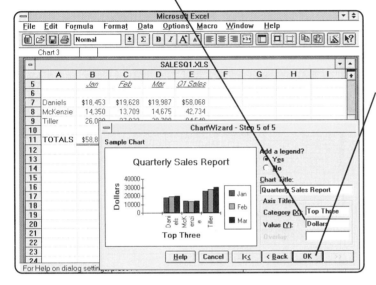

Notice that "Dollars" appears on the left of the chart.

5. **Click** on **OK**. The Quarterly Sales Report column chart will appear on your worksheet.

Congratulations. You have created an embedded column chart! An *embedded* chart is a permanent part of your worksheet. Any time you make a change in your worksheet data, the change is reflected in this chart.

CHANGING THE VIEW

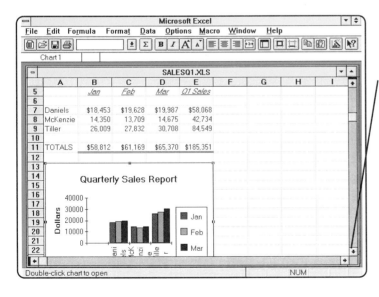

1. **Click repeatedly** on ↓ on the scroll bar to bring the entire chart into view if you cannot see all of it.

Notice that the names of the salespeople are vertical and look funny. You will remedy that in the next chapter.

SAVING THE COLUMN CHART

1. **Click** on **File** in the menu bar. A pull-down menu will appear.

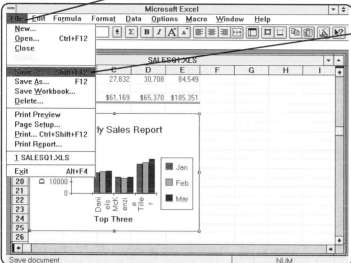

2. **Click** on **Save**. The pull-down menu will disappear. Your chart is now saved as part of the SALESQ1 worksheet.

Oops... Accidents Will Happen!

If you accidentally clicked on the chart area before you clicked on Save, the Save As dialog box will appear with the name Chart 1 highlighted in the File Name text box. Since you are saving Chart 1 as part of the worksheet and not as an independent file, you will need to cancel.

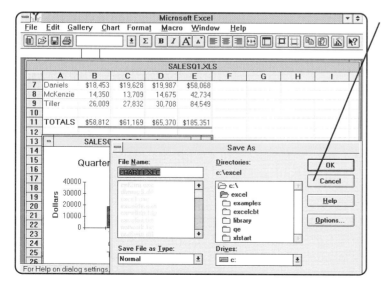

1. **Click** on **Cancel**. The Save As dialog box will disappear.

2. **Click twice anywhere** on the **worksheet** (but not on the chart). The chart will look like what you see in the example above.

3. **Repeat steps 1 and 2** in the previous section to save the worksheet and the chart together.

Working with Legends and Axis Text

A *legend* on a map tells you what the symbols on a map mean. The chart legend in the example in this chapter tells you the meaning of the various colors of the chart columns. *Axis text* are the labels on either the X or Y axis. The X axis text in the example in this chapter lists the salespeople's names. In this chapter you will:

❖ Change the orientation of text on the X axis so it prints horizontally

❖ Make a chart larger

❖ Change the legend text

❖ Move a legend to a new location on the chart

❖ Delete and restore a legend

CHANGING THE ORIENTATION OF TEXT ON THE X AXIS

In this section, you will change the strange way the salespeople's names appear on the X axis of the chart you created in Chapter 17.

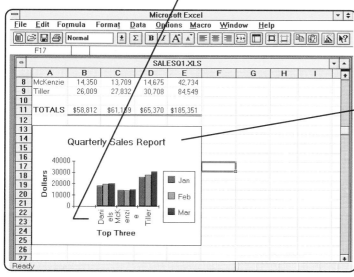

1. Open the **SALESQ1 worksheet** with Chart 1 if it is not already on your screen.

2. Click twice anywhere on the **chart**. The chart will become an active window with its own title bar. Your window view may look like one of the views shown in the next three examples.

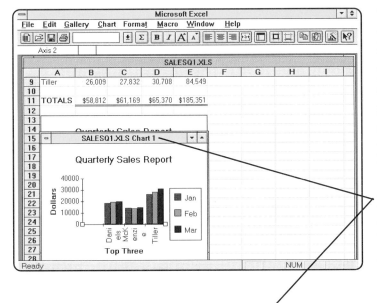

The two examples on this page represent possible views you may see when you click twice on the chart. The view that you see depends on where your chart was positioned before you clicked. Any of the views is correct.

Notice the active title bars on the Chart 1 windows in both of these views as well as in the one at the top of the next page.

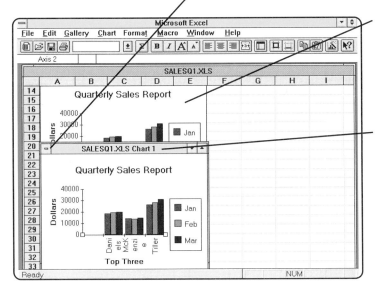

Notice the chart in the background of the examples on this page. This is the embedded chart that you created.

Notice the embedded chart's active window is in the foreground. This is the edit window of the embedded chart in the background.

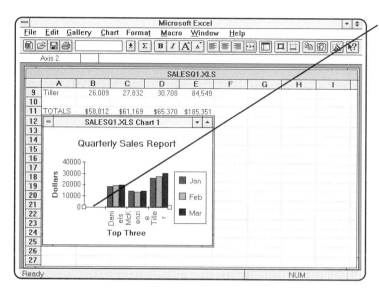

3. Click on the **X axis** (the horizontal line representing the productivity of the three top salespeople).

White squares (called *handles*) appear at each end of the axis after you click on it. *This can be a very tricky operation. The goal is to have only two white handles, one at each end of the X axis,* as shown here. If you end up with white handles all over the place, don't be discouraged. Just keep clicking on the X axis on the chart until you get only two white handles, one at each end.

4. Click on **Format** in the menu bar. A pull-down menu will appear.

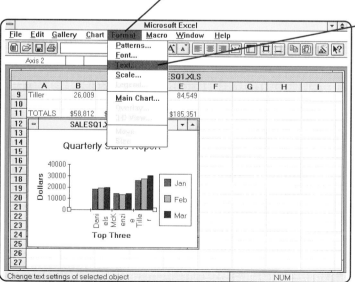

5. Click on **Text**. The Text dialog box will appear.

Note: If the Text option on the pull-down menu is grayed out, check to see if the X axis has two white handles on it, one at each end. If it doesn't, repeat step 3 above.

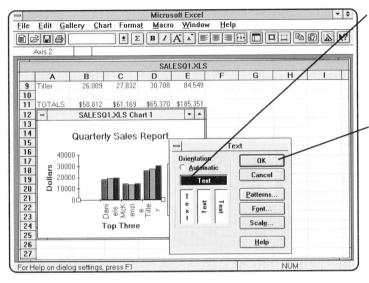

6. Click on **Text** in the horizontal option box. The box background will turn black and the text will become white.

7. Click on **OK**. The Text dialog box will disappear. The names of the salespeople will appear horizontally on the chart.

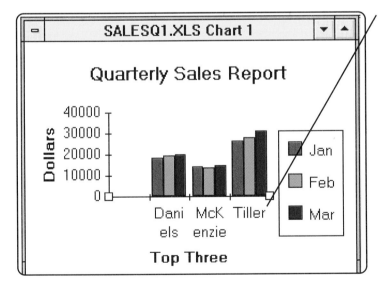

Notice that the names still look funny. Don't worry. In the next section you will get the chance to fix them when you enlarge the chart.

Your funny looking names may have a slightly different arrangement. It all depends on how precise you were in setting up the chart workspace in Chapter 17.

ENLARGING A CHART

To enlarge a chart you must first get out of the active window/title bar mode.

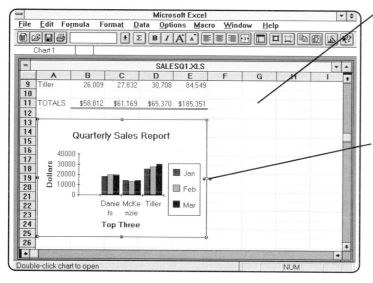

1. **Click once anywhere** on the **worksheet**. The title bar will disappear and the chart will be surrounded by a border with black selection handles.

2. **Move** the pointer to the **center handle** on the **right border** of the chart. The pointer will change to a two-headed arrow.

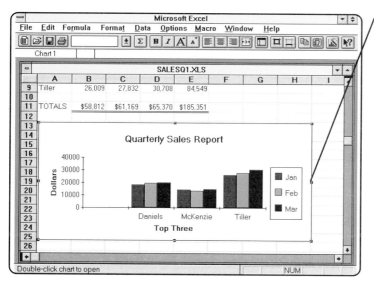

3. **Press and hold** the mouse button and **drag** the border by the handle to the **end of column H**. You will see an outline of the chart expand as you drag.

4. **Release** the mouse button. The chart will expand to fill the space. The names of the top three salespeople will be spaced normally.

CHANGING THE LEGEND TEXT

Legend text on the chart is determined by the text on the worksheet. To change the text on the legend you change the text on the worksheet. In this section you will change Jan, Feb, and Mar to January, February, and March. You'll also see how versatile the AutoFill feature is.

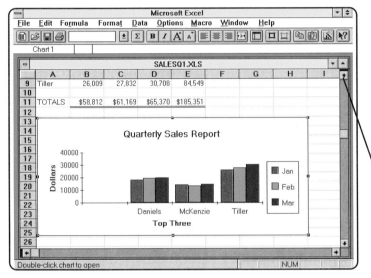

1. **Click repeatedly** on the ⬆ on the scroll bar to go up to row 5 and bring Jan, Feb, and Mar into view.

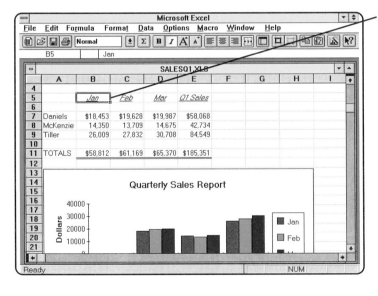

2. **Click** on Jan in **B5** to select the cell.

3. **Type January**.

4. **Press Enter**.

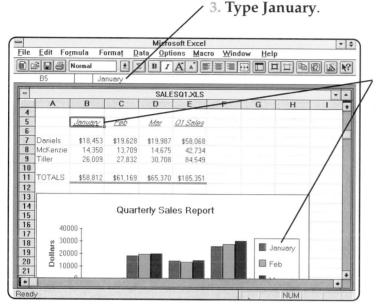

Notice that the word January is entered into cell B5 of the worksheet and into the legend on the chart at the same time.

5. **Move** the mouse pointer to the **small square** (called the *fill handle*) in the lower-right corner of the cell border. The pointer will change to a black plus sign.

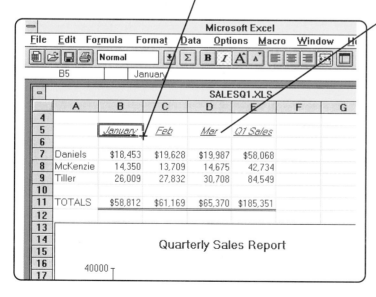

6. **Press and hold** the mouse button as you **drag** the fill handle across Mar in **D5**.

7. **Release** the mouse button. "Feb" and "Mar" will change automatically to "February" and "March." The change will appear in the legend on the chart at the same time.

MOVING A LEGEND

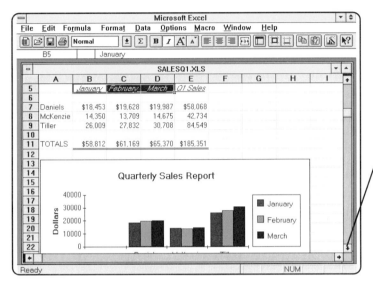

In this section you will move the legend to the bottom of the chart. You need to make room for it at the bottom so you will enlarge the chart to fill the space A13:H33.

1. Click repeatedly on the ⬇ on the scroll bar to bring the chart into full view.

2. Click once anywhere on the **chart**. It will be surrounded by a border with selection handles.

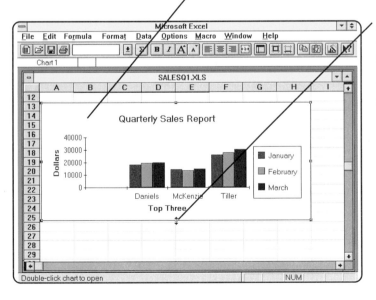

3. Move the mouse pointer to the **center handle** at the bottom of the chart. It will change to a two-headed arrow.

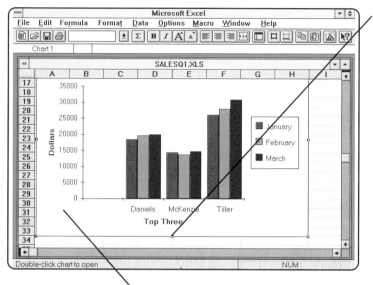

4. **Press and hold** the mouse button and **drag** the border with the handle to **row 33**. The screen will scroll down to show more rows as you drag the handle.

5. **Release** the mouse button. The chart will expand to fill the space.

You are now ready to change the position of the legend. Since you are changing something on the chart itself, you must switch the chart to an active (or edit) window with a title bar.

6. **Click twice anywhere** on the **chart**. It will change to an active window with a title bar.

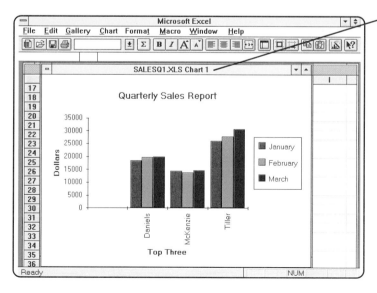

Your screen may look like this example. If it doesn't, it may look like the one at the top of the next page. You may even have a variation of the one at the top of the next page. As long as the chart window has a title bar, it's okay.

The chart view at the bottom of the previous page is the view most people will see. However, some people get the view shown here, or a variation of it. We checked with Microsoft's support personnel. They seem to think it may have to do with the mysterious inner workings of some video cards. Why this happens is really not important. What is important is that you have an active Chart 1 window with a title bar.

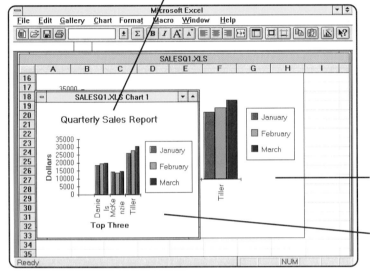

Notice the embedded chart in the background.

Notice the active chart window in the foreground.

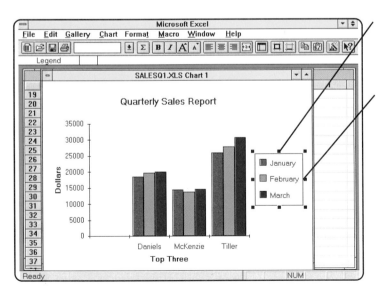

7. **Click** on the **legend box**. It will be surrounded by a border with black handles.

Notice the black handles. If you get white handles, continue to click until you get black ones.

8. **Click** on **Format** in the menu bar. A pull-down menu will appear.

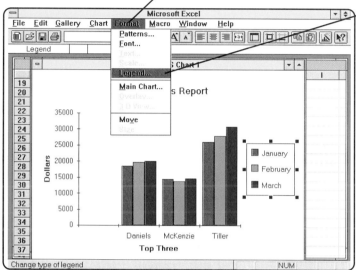

9. **Click** on **Legend**. The Legend dialog box will appear.

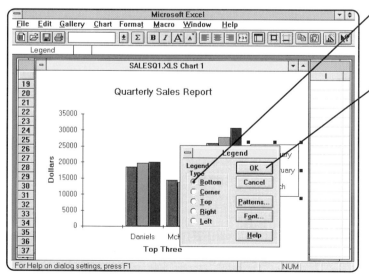

10. **Click** on **Bottom** to insert a black dot in the circle.

11. **Click** on **OK**. The legend will be moved to the bottom of the chart. Depending on the size of the chart in your view, the Y axis numbers on the scale may change. The numbers in the Y axis scale change to make room for the legend on the bottom.

DELETING A LEGEND

Before you can delete a legend you must select it. If you have been following the steps in this chapter, the legend is already surrounded by a border with selection handles. If it is not, click on it.

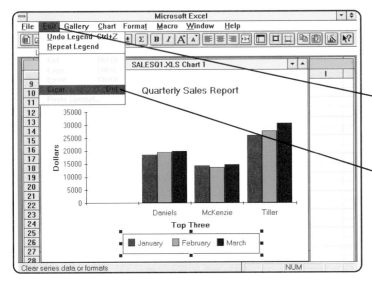

1. **Click** on **Edit** in the menu bar. A pull-down menu will appear.

2. **Click** on **Clear**. The legend will disappear.

You will restore the legend in the next section.

RESTORING A LEGEND

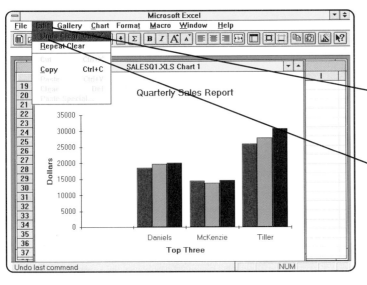

This procedure works only if deleting the legend was the last thing you did.

1. **Click** on **Edit** in the menu bar. A pull-down menu will appear.

2. **Click** on **Undo Clear**. The pull-down menu will disappear and the legend box will reappear at the bottom of the chart.

SAVING CHANGES
IN A CHART

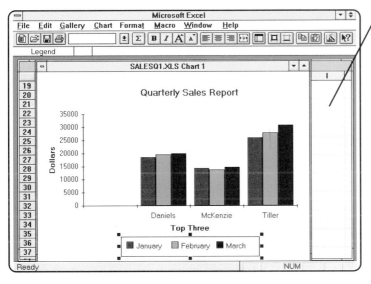

1. Click once anywhere off the **chart**. The title bar will disappear and the embedded chart will appear with black handles on the border.

If by chance your chart has filled the screen and no part of the worksheet is showing as it is in this example, **click once** on the **SALESQ1.XLS title bar**. (You will not have the SALESQ1.XLS title bar unless your chart fills the screen.) The embedded chart will appear with a border around it.

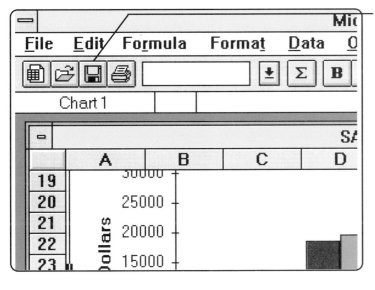

2. Click on the **Save tool** in the toolbar. You won't see any difference in your screen, but the worksheet with the edited chart is now saved.

Printing Charts

You can print a chart by itself or on the same page with a worksheet. You can also print a chart and a worksheet sideways. Printing sideways is called printing in *landscape* orientation. In this chapter you will:

❖ Print a chart

❖ Print a chart and a worksheet on the same page

❖ Preview and print a chart and a worksheet sideways (in landscape orientation)

PRINTING A CHART

In this section you will print only a chart.

1. Open the **SALESQ1 worksheet** with Chart 1 if it is not already on your screen.

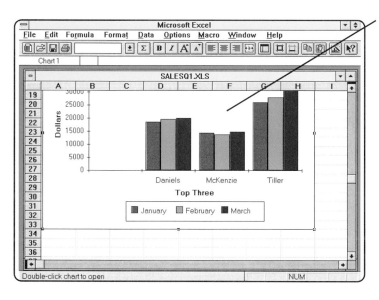

2. Click twice anywhere on the **chart**. The chart will become an active window with a title bar.

3. **Click** on the **Print tool** on the toolbar. The Printing message box will appear. The SALESQ1.XLS Chart 1 will be printed.

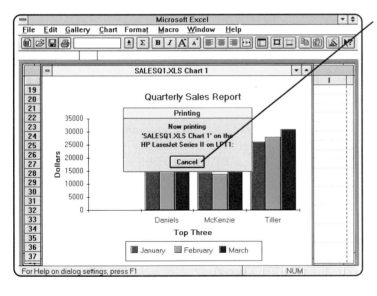

Note: If you chose the Print Preview option in Chapter 5, the Print Preview will appear. In that case, **click** on the **Print button** on the Print Preview screen menu bar. The SALESQ1.XLS Chart 1 will be printed.

4. If you change your mind, **click** on **Cancel**.

PRINTING A WORKSHEET AND CHART AT THE SAME TIME

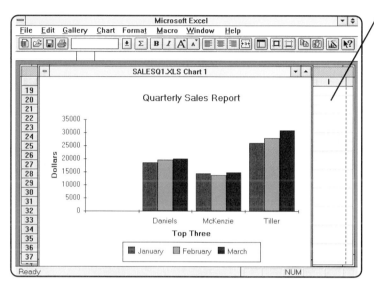

1. **Click once anywhere** on the **worksheet**. The chart title bar will disappear.

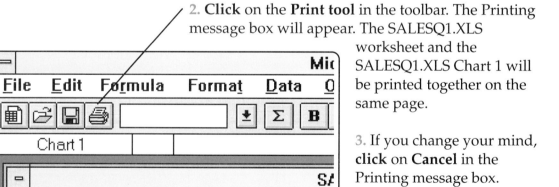

2. **Click** on the **Print tool** in the toolbar. The Printing message box will appear. The SALESQ1.XLS worksheet and the SALESQ1.XLS Chart 1 will be printed together on the same page.

3. If you change your mind, **click** on **Cancel** in the Printing message box.

PRINTING A WORKSHEET AND CHART SIDEWAYS

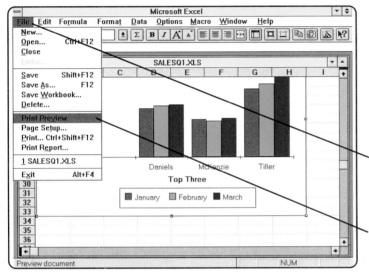

There may be a time when you will want to print both a worksheet and a chart sideways (in *landscape* orientation) on your paper, especially if your worksheet is quite wide.

1. **Click** on **File** in the menu bar. A pull-down menu will appear.

2. **Click** on **Print Preview**. The Print Preview screen will appear.

Most documents are normally printed in *portrait* orientation, with the short side of the paper at the top. This is what you will see the first time you select the Print Preview option. This preview is an example of a portrait orientation.

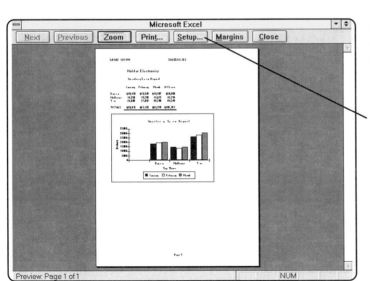

3. **Click** on **Setup**. The Page Setup dialog box will appear.

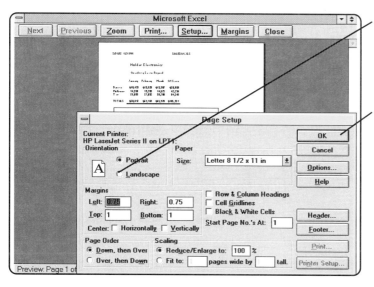

4. Click on the **Landscape circle** in the Orientation option box to place a black dot inside the circle.

5. Click on **OK**. The preview screen will reappear. This time the page view will be in landscape orientation.

Landscape printing means printing with the long side of the paper on top. Landscape printing is often used to print financial worksheets and charts that are too wide to be printed in portrait.

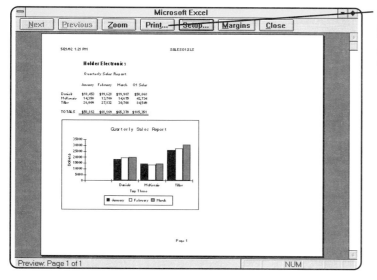

6. Click on **Print**. The Page Setup dialog box will disappear. The Print dialog box will appear.

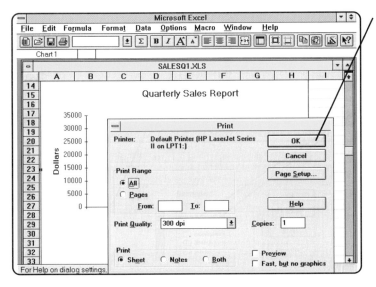

7. Click on **OK**. The Printing message box will appear. The worksheet and chart will be printed sideways.

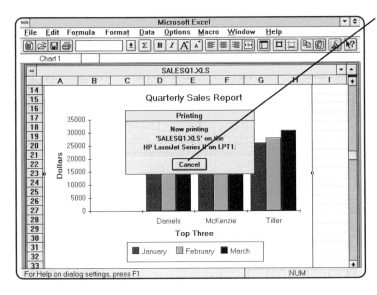

If you want to cancel the printing job before it happens, **click** on **Cancel**.

Switching Back to Portrait Printing

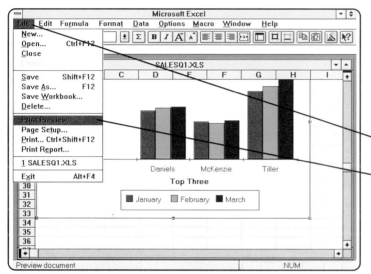

It is a good idea to switch back to portrait printing at this time. Otherwise, the next time you print something it will be printed sideways.

1. **Click** on **File**.

2. **Click** on **Print Preview**. The Print Preview screen will appear. The preview window will show the worksheet in landscape orientation.

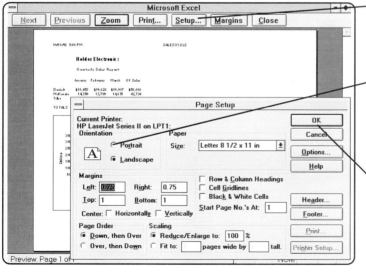

3. **Click** on **Setup**. The Page Setup dialog box will reappear.

4. **Click** on the **Portrait circle** in the Orientation option box to place a black dot inside the circle.

5. **Click** on **OK**. The Print Preview screen will appear. The preview window will show the worksheet in portrait orientation.

Your printer will now print in portrait.

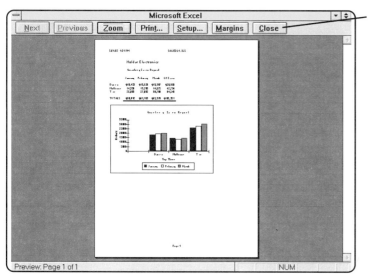

6. **Click** on **Close**. The SALESQ1.XLS screen will appear.

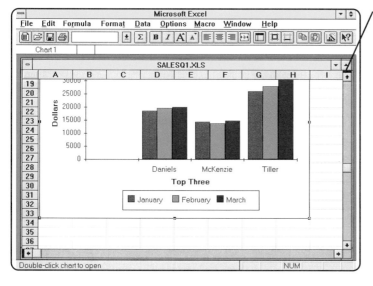

7. **Click repeatedly** on ⬆ on the scroll bar to bring the entire chart into view.

If you are going on to Chapter 20, you need not exit or save at this time.

Saving, Deleting, and Restoring a Chart

If you have a large worksheet, you may want to remove the chart from the worksheet and store it in its own file. One of the exciting features of Excel is that you can save a chart to a separate file and then remove it from the worksheet. A chart saved to its own separate file continues to be linked to the worksheet. Any changes made in the worksheet will be automatically reflected in the chart. You can also restore a deleted chart file to your worksheet at any time. In this chapter you will:

❖ Save a chart to a separate file

❖ Delete the chart from the worksheet

❖ Restore the chart to the worksheet

SAVING A CHART TO A FILE

1. **Click twice anywhere** on the **chart** (not on the worksheet). The chart will become an active window entitled "SALESQ1.XLS Chart 1."

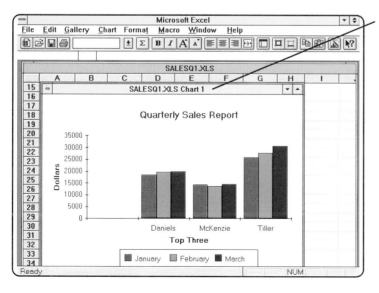

Notice the active window title bar that appears after you click twice on the chart. Your active window view may be different from this. The key point is that you have a SALESQ1.XLS Chart 1 title bar.

2. **Click** on **File** in the menu bar. A pull-down menu will appear.

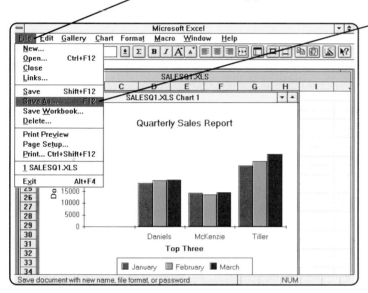

3. **Click** on **Save As**. The Save As dialog box will appear.

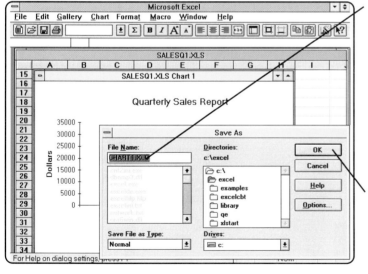

Notice the name CHART1.XLC is highlighted in the File Name text box. This is the name Excel will automatically give to the chart unless you change it. In this example, you will use the name.

4. **Click** on **OK**. A copy of the SALESQ1.XLS Chart 1 is now saved in a separate file entitled CHART1.XLC.

DELETING A CHART
FROM A WORKSHEET

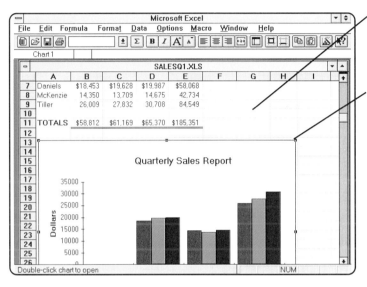

1. **Click once anywhere** on the **worksheet** (not on the chart).

The chart will become surrounded by a border with selection handles.

2. Click on **Edit** in the menu bar. A pull-down menu will appear.

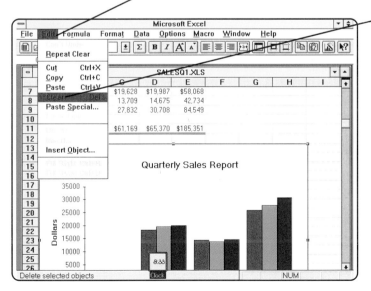

3. Click on **Clear**. The chart will disappear.

Don't panic! You still have a copy of the chart in a separate file. Moreover, you can view or restore the chart to the worksheet at any time by following the steps in the next section.

RESTORING A DELETED CHART TO A WORKSHEET

In this section you will open the CHART1.XLC file and copy it to the Windows Clipboard. Then you will paste a copy of the chart from the Clipboard into the SALESQ1.XLS worksheet.

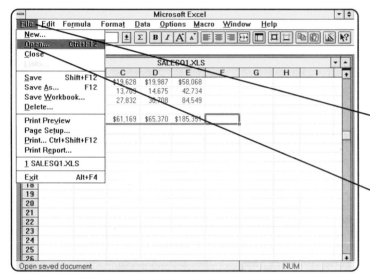

Copying CHART1.XLC to the Clipboard

1. **Click** on **File** in the menu bar. A pull-down menu will appear.

2. **Click** on **Open**. The Open dialog box will appear.

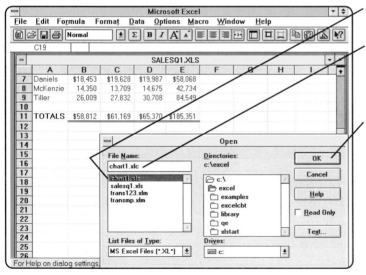

3. **Click** on **chart1.xlc**.

The filename, chart1.xlc, will appear in the File Name text box.

4. **Click** on **OK**. The CHART1.XLC window will appear.

5. Click on **Edit** in the menu bar. A pull-down menu will appear.

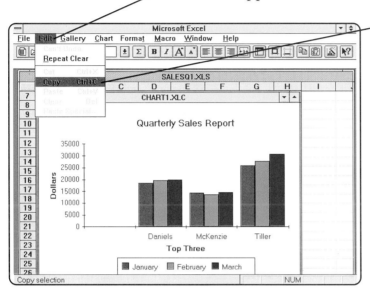

6. Click on **Copy**. The chart will be surrounded by a moving border. It is now copied to the Windows Clipboard.

Opening the SALESQ1.XLS Worksheet File

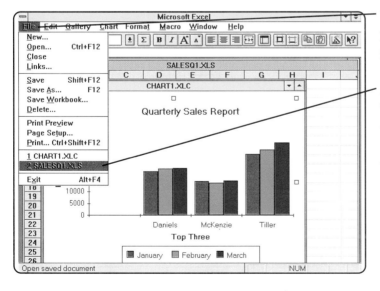

1. Click on **File** in the menu bar. A pull-down menu will appear.

2. Click on **SALESQ1.XLS**. The CHART1.XLC window will disappear and the SALESQ1.XLS worksheet will appear.

Pasting the Chart Back into the Worksheet

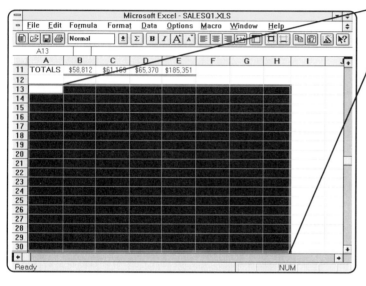

1. Click on cell **A13**. Leave the cursor in the cell.

2. Press and hold the left mouse button as you **drag** it to cell **H32**. Your screen will move up as you approach H32 and the TOTALS row will disappear.

3. Release the mouse button when you have highlighted the range A13 to H32.

4. Click on **Edit** in the menu bar. A pull-down menu will appear.

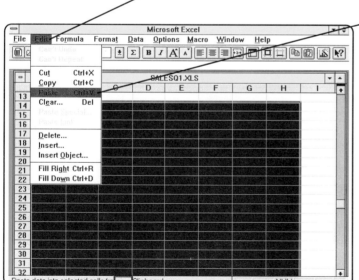

5. Click on **Paste**. The pull-down menu will disappear. The Quarterly Sales Report chart (CHART1.XLC) will appear on the worksheet in the area that you highlighted in steps 1 to 3 above.

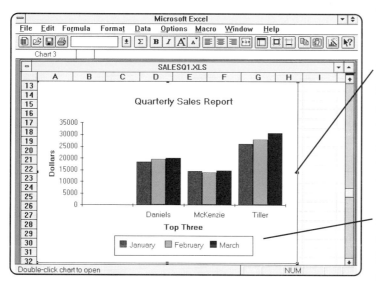

Terrific! You have restored the chart to the worksheet!

Notice that the Quarterly Sales Report chart is surrounded by a border with handles. This means it is now the active area in the SALESQ1.XLS worksheet.

6. Click twice anywhere on the **chart**. The SALESQ1.XLS Chart 2 active window will appear.

Notice that the Quarterly Sales Report active window is now labeled "Chart 2." When you restore a deleted chart to a worksheet (or create another chart on the worksheet), that chart is assigned the next number in the sequence. There is nothing you can do about this situation. It's the way Excel is programmed. In this example, however, Chart 2 is exactly the same as Chart 1 in all respects except for the name. Any change you make in the worksheet will be automatically reflected in both Chart 1.XLC and in Chart 2.

In the next chapter you will learn to edit text, add new text, and use the drawing toolbar. If you plan to go on to the next chapter now, leave the chart window as it is in this example.

Adding and Editing Chart Text, Arrows, and Shapes

In Excel *attached text* is text that is permanently linked to a chart, like the X axis title, "Top Three," in Chart 2 below. You can add attached text to charts and edit it. You can also place and move *unattached text* anywhere on a chart. Similarly, arrows and other drawings can be added and placed anywhere on a chart. In this chapter you will:

❖ Edit attached text on a chart

❖ Add unattached text to emphasize the top salesperson

❖ Draw an oval to encircle the unattached text

❖ Draw an arrow to point to the highest column on the chart

EDITING ATTACHED CHART TEXT

1. **Open** the **SALESQ1.XLS worksheet** containing Chart 2 that you created in Chapter 20. Refer to Chapter 7, "Opening a Saved File," if you need help. If you have

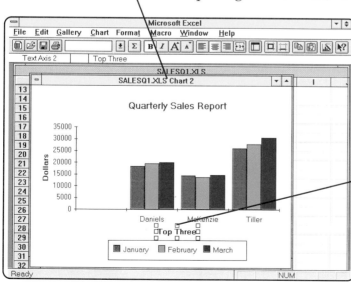

been following along in the chapters, Chart 2 should look like the one shown here. If it does not have a title bar, **click twice anywhere** on the **chart**. The SALESQ1.XLS Chart 2 window will appear.

2. **Click** on **Top Three**, the X axis text at the bottom of the chart. It will become surrounded by white handles.

3. **Move** the mouse pointer to the **formula bar**.

4. **Click** on the space just to the **right** of the word **Three** to set the cursor.

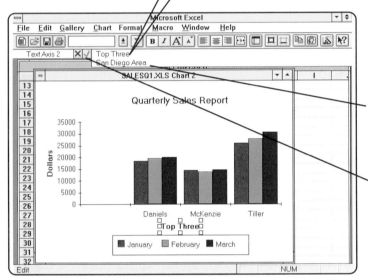

5. **Press and hold** the **Alt** key and **press** the **Enter** key (Alt + Enter) to insert another line in the text box.

6. **Type San Diego Area**. This text will appear under the text "Top Three."

7. **Click** on ✔ or **press Enter** to insert the second line of text under "Top Three."

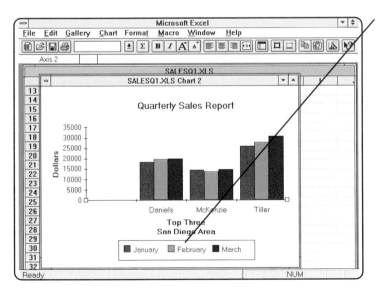

Notice that the legend automatically moved down to make room for the additional line of text. Isn't this a great feature?

ADDING UNATTACHED TEXT

1. **Press Esc.** The chart will be cleared of all handles. It is important that you have *no handles* showing, otherwise step 2 will not work.

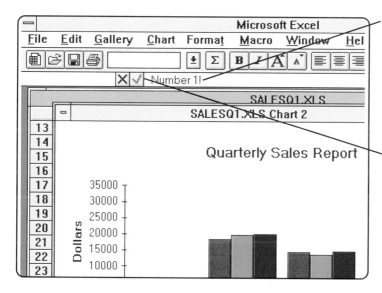

2. **Type Number 1!** As you begin to type, the letters will show up in the formula bar. The Cancel box (✗) and the Enter box (✔) will appear.

3. **Click** on ✔ or **press Enter**. The text will appear on the chart surrounded by black handles.

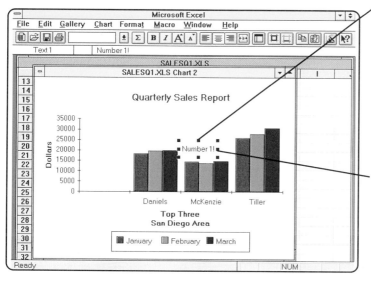

Notice that the unattached text box mysteriously placed itself in this location. Your text box may end up in a different place. The next step will be to move it into a better location.

4. **Click** on the **text box**.

5. **Press and hold** the mouse button. "Number 1!" will be surrounded by a box.

6. While still pressing and holding the mouse button, **drag** the **box** to a place on the chart where you want the "Number 1!" text to appear. The "Number 1!" text itself will not move until you release the mouse button. In the next section you will draw an ellipse around the text. In the section following it you will draw an arrow from the text to Tiller's columns. Place the text so there is room for the ellipse and arrow.

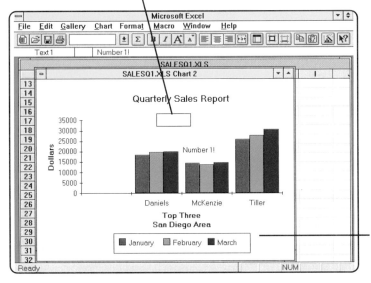

7. **Release** the mouse button. The text will move to the new location.

8. **Click** on **any blank spot** on the **chart**. The black handles will disappear.

DRAWING AN OVAL AROUND THE TEXT

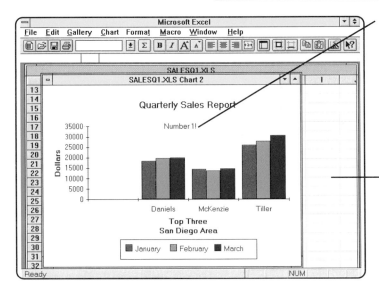

Notice the new location of the unattached text.

Opening the Drawing Toolbar

1. **Click once anywhere** on the **worksheet** (not on the chart). The chart will become surrounded by a border with black handles.

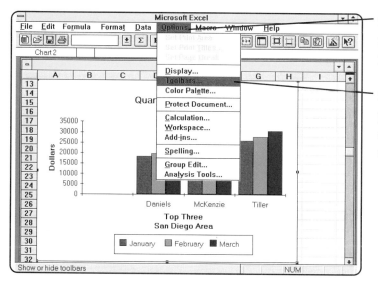

2. Click on **Options** in the menu bar. A pull-down menu will appear.

3. Click on **Toolbars**. The pull-down menu will disappear. The Toolbars dialog box will appear.

4. Click on **Drawing**.

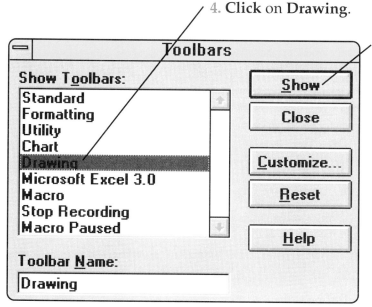

5. Click on **Show**. The Drawing toolbar will appear in a small window. It will choose its own location on the screen. Yours may be in a different place than the one shown in the examples on the next page.

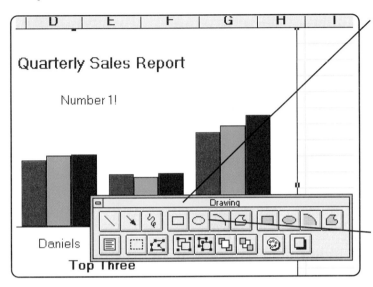

If you want to move the location of the toolbar window, **move** the mouse pointer to the **Drawing title bar, press and hold** the mouse button as you **drag** the toolbar to a **new location**.

Drawing an Oval

1. Click on the **Oval tool**. The cursor will turn into a black crosshair.

2. Move the crosshair to an area just to the **left** and **above** the text, **"Number 1!"**

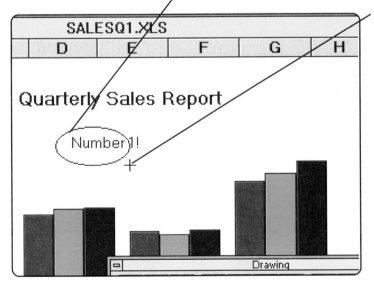

3. Press and hold the mouse button as you **drag** the crosshair **down** and to the **right**.

Notice that an oval will form as you drag the crosshair. The idea is to surround "Number 1!" with the oval.

4. **Release** the mouse button. The text will be surrounded by an oval. The oval itself will be surrounded by black handles.

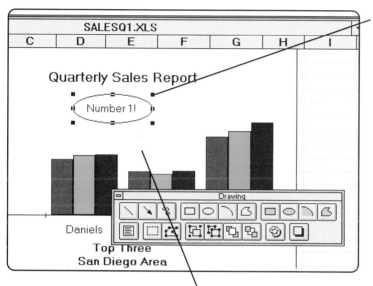

To change the size and shape of the oval, put your mouse pointer on any handle. The pointer will change to a two-headed arrow. **Press and hold** the mouse button as you **drag** the handle. Drag toward the middle of the oval to make the oval smaller. Drag out to make it larger. You may have to fiddle with it to get it to look the way you want.

5. **Click once anywhere** on the **chart**. The black handles will disappear. "Number 1!" will be surrounded by an oval.

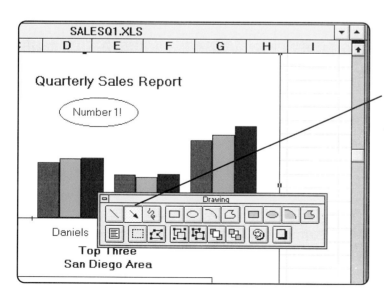

ADDING AN ARROW

1. **Click** on the **Arrow tool**. The cursor will turn into a black crosshair.

2. **Move** the **crosshair** to the **right** edge of the **oval**.

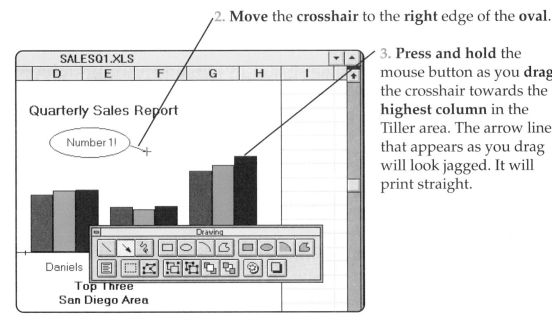

3. **Press and hold** the mouse button as you **drag** the crosshair towards the **highest column** in the Tiller area. The arrow line that appears as you drag will look jagged. It will print straight.

4. **Release** the mouse button. The arrowhead will be added to the arrow line.

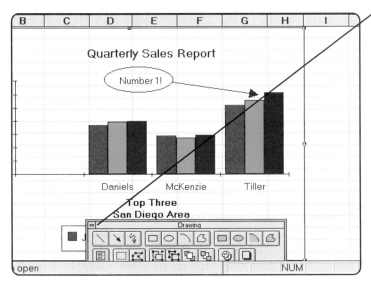

5. **Click once** on the **Control menu box** (⊟) on the left of the Drawing title bar. The drawing toolbar will disappear.

Isn't this great? You now have a terrific looking column chart. If you want to get even more sophisticated, complete the next two chapters!

Changing Fonts on a Chart

There is a trick to changing the chart fonts in Excel. Excel treats the text that is linked with the chart (attached text) differently from the text that you added to the chart (unattached text). In this chapter you will:

❖ Change the font of the *attached* text "Quarterly Sales Report"

❖ Change the font of the *unattached* text "Number 1!"

❖ Change the font of the names of the salespeople. This attached text is a part of the X axis description

CHANGING THE FONT OF ATTACHED TEXT

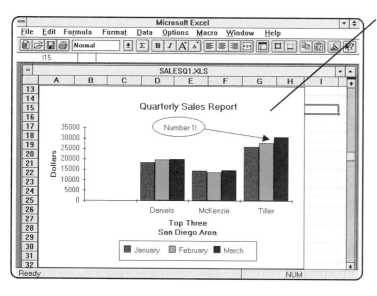

1. Click twice anywhere on the **chart**. The SALESQ1 Chart 2 window will appear.

Notice that the arrow and the oval that you created in Chapter 21 are not visible. For some mysterious reason, the shapes and arrows created with the drawing tools are programmed to be part of the worksheet and not part of the embedded chart. This means that when you copy or link this chart to a word processed document (as shown in Chapters 24 and 25), arrows and shapes are not copied.

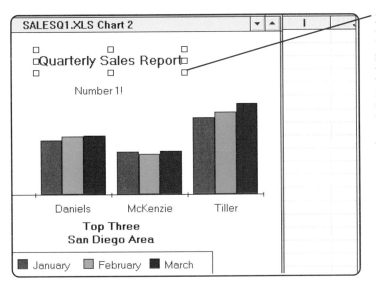

2. **Click** on **Quarterly Sales Report**. The text will be surrounded by white handles. If the text is not surrounded by these handles, you will not be able to accomplish step 3 below.

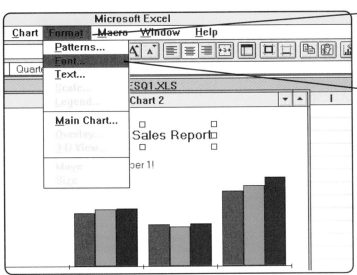

3. **Click** on **Format** in the menu bar. A pull-down menu will appear.

4. **Click** on **Font**. The Font dialog box will appear.

Notice the current font is MS Sans Serif, that its style is Bold, and its size is 12 points.

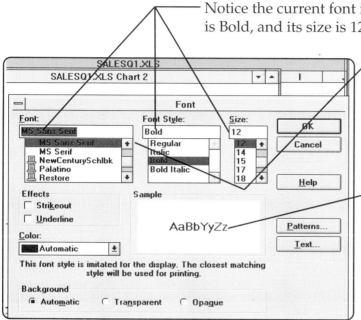

5. Click repeatedly on ⬆ on the scroll bar in the Font list box until you reach the Arial font. If you do not have this font, pick one you like.

Notice the Sample view of this font.

6. Click on **Arial**. It will become highlighted and "Arial" will appear in the Font text box. Since the style is already Bold, you do not have to click on Bold.

7. Click on **14**. It will become highlighted and "14" will appear in the Size text box.

Notice how the font changes in the Sample box as you change font and size.

8. Click on **OK**. The Font dialog box will disappear. The chart window will come to the foreground and the font for the text, "Quarterly Sales Report," will change to Arial, Bold, 14 points.

CHANGING THE FONT OF UNATTACHED TEXT

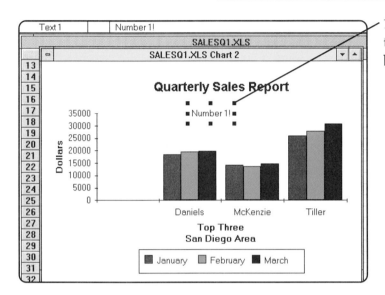

1. **Click** on **Number 1!** The text will be surrounded by black handles.

2. **Click** on **Format** in the menu bar. A pull-down menu will appear.

3. **Click** on **Font**. The Font dialog box will appear.

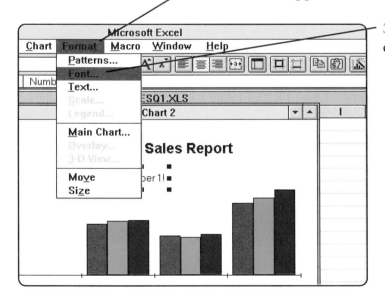

Notice the current font is MS Sans Serif, that its style is Regular, and its size is 10 points.

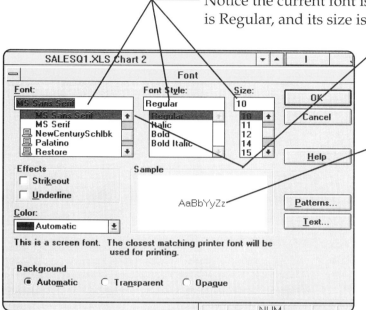

4. Click repeatedly on ⬆ on the scroll bar in the Font list box until you reach the Arial font.

Notice the sample view of the MS Sans Serif font.

5. **Click** on **Arial**. It will become highlighted and "Arial" will appear in the Font text box.

6. **Click** on **Bold**. It will become highlighted and "Bold" will appear in the Font Style text box.

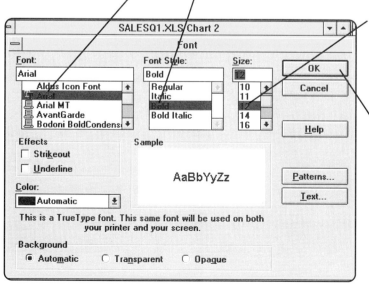

7. **Click** on **12**. It will become highlighted and "12" will appear in the Size text box.

8. **Click** on **OK**. The Font dialog box will disappear. The chart window will come to the foreground and the font for the text, "Number 1!," will change to Arial, Bold, 12 points.

Resizing the Oval to Fit the Larger Font

When you enlarged the font for the text, "Number 1!," it became too large to fit in the oval. This section will show you how to fix it.

1. Click anywhere on the **worksheet** (off the chart). The chart window will disappear. The chart will be surrounded by a border with black handles.

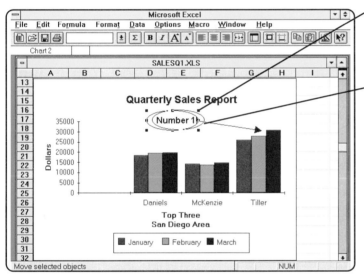

2. Click on the **edge** of the **oval**. It will be surrounded by black handles.

3. Press and hold the mouse button as you **drag** the oval to size it to fit the larger font. As you drag to enlarge the oval, you will see both ovals.

4. Release the mouse button. The original oval will disappear and a new, larger oval will appear. You may have to fiddle with it to get it enlarged and positioned into the shape and size you want.

Resizing and Positioning the Arrow to Fit the Larger Font

When you enlarged the oval in the previous section, the arrow was no longer the correct length. This example will show you how to resize the arrow to fit the space between the larger oval and the Tiller March column.

1. **Click anywhere** on the **arrow**. A black handle will appear at each end.

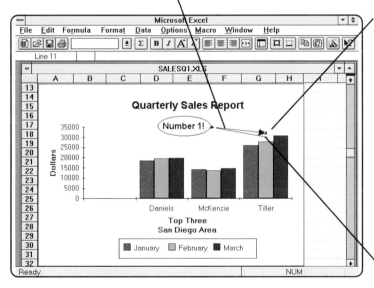

2. **Press and hold** the mouse button as you **drag** the arrow to realign it.

3. **Release** the mouse button. The arrow will assume its new position. You may have to fiddle with it to get it positioned correctly. You may also have to shorten or lengthen the arrow to make it fit.

4. To shorten or lengthen the arrow, **click** on a **black handle** at the end of the arrow, and **press and hold** as you **drag** the handle to shorten or lengthen the arrow.

5. **Release** the mouse button. The arrow will assume its new length. You may have to fiddle with it to get it the way you want it.

CHANGING THE
X AXIS TEXT FONT

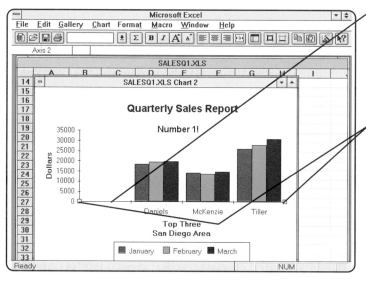

1. **Click** on the **X axis**. This is the axis that contains the last names of the top three salespeople used in this example.

Notice that white handles will appear on each end of the X axis. If these handles are not present on each end, you will not be able to change or style the font.

2. **Click** on **Format** in the menu bar. A pull-down menu will appear.

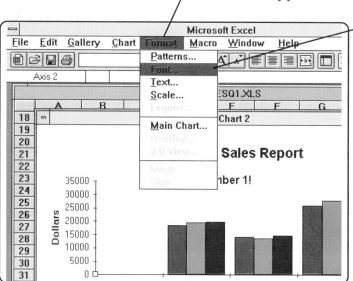

3. **Click** on **Font**. The Font dialog box will appear.

Notice the current font is MS Sans Serif, that its style is Regular, and its size is 10 points.

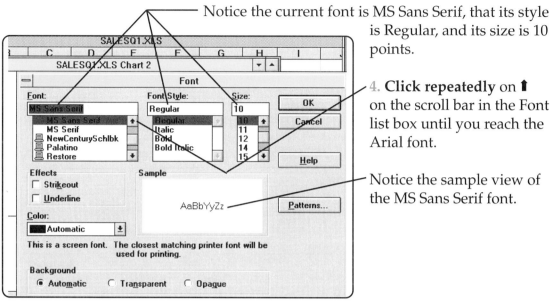

4. Click repeatedly on ⬆ on the scroll bar in the Font list box until you reach the Arial font.

Notice the sample view of the MS Sans Serif font.

5. Click on **Arial**. It will become highlighted and "Arial" will appear in the Font Style text box.

6. Click on **Bold**. It will become highlighted and "Bold" will appear in the Font Style text box.

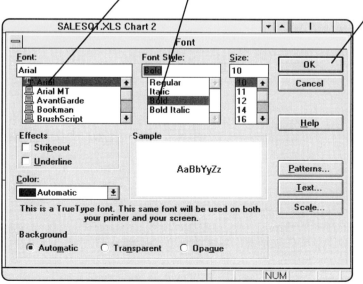

7. Click on **OK**. The Font dialog box will disappear. The chart window will come to the foreground and the font for the last names of the three salespeople will change to Arial, Bold, 10 points.

8. Click anywhere on the **worksheet** (off the chart). The chart window will disappear. The chart will be surrounded by a border with black handles.

Congratulations. You have mastered the art of changing fonts!

SUMMARY
OF THE FONT CHANGES
MADE IN THIS CHAPTER

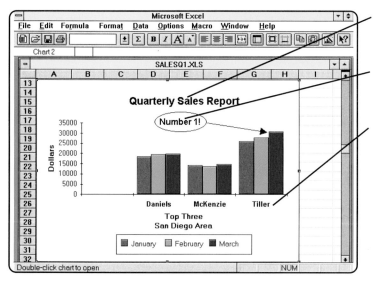

"Quarterly Sales Report" is now Arial, Bold, 14 points.

"Number 1!" is now Arial, Bold, 12 points.

The names are now Arial, Bold, 10 points.

Adding a Border and Patterns to a Chart

In Excel the options available for styling your chart can be mind boggling. If you are printing in black and white, the Patterns option improves a chart's appearance immensely. If you have a color printer, your styling options are even greater! In this chapter you will:

❖ Add a color border to the chart

❖ Add patterns to the columns

❖ Restore the original patterns to the columns

ADDING A BORDER TO A CHART

1. **Click once anywhere** on the **chart**. (Make certain you don't click twice.)

The chart will be surrounded by a border with black handles.

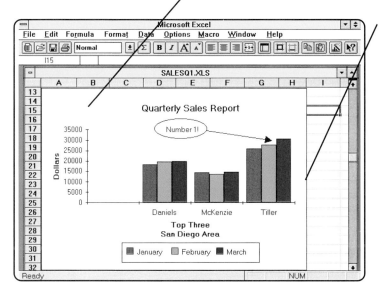

2. Click on **Format** in the menu bar. A pull-down menu will appear.

3. Click on **Patterns**. The Patterns dialog box will appear.

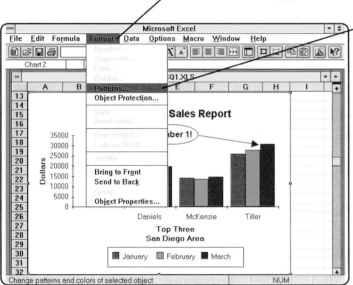

4. Click on the **Custom circle** in the Border option box to place a black dot in the circle.

5. Click on ⬇ to the **right** of the **Color list box**. A drop-down list of optional border colors will appear.

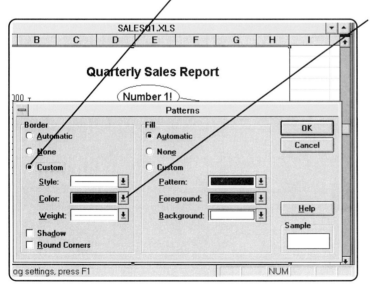

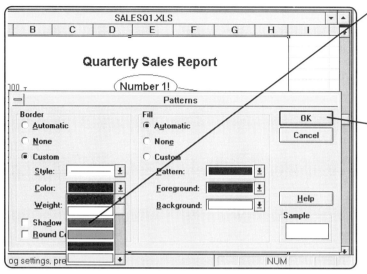

6. **Click** on the **red color option box**. The drop-down list will disappear. The red color will appear in the Color list box.

7. **Click** on **OK**. The Patterns dialog box will disappear. The chart will be surrounded by a red border.

Neat.

ADDING PATTERNS TO A CHART

1. **Click twice anywhere** on the **chart**. The SALESQ1.XLS Chart 2 window will appear.

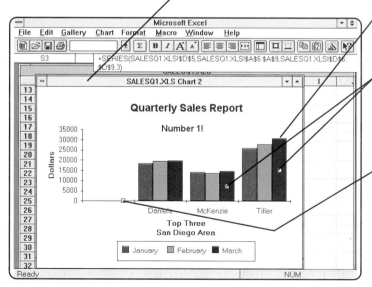

2. **Click** on **Tiller's March column**.

Notice that white handles appear on the March columns of two of the three salespeople.

Notice a third white handle appears on the X axis line. If you get a different set of white handles, keep clicking on the March columns until you duplicate the view here.

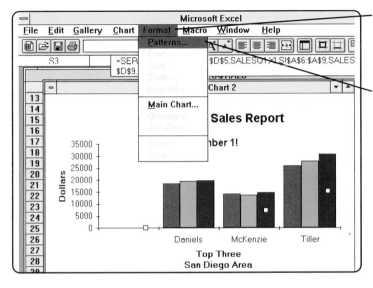

3. **Click** on **Format** in the menu bar. A pull-down menu will appear.

4. **Click** on **Patterns**. The Patterns dialog box will appear.

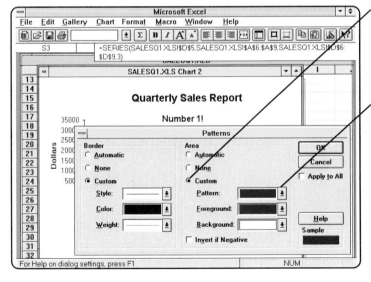

5. **Click** on the **Custom circle** in the Area option box to place a black dot in the circle.

6. **Click** on ⬇ to the **right** of the **Pattern list box**. A drop-down list of optional color patterns will appear.

7. **Click repeatedly** on ⬇ to scroll down the list until you find a pattern you would like to put on the March columns.

8. **Click** on the **pattern** you like. Your pattern choice may be different from the one shown here.

9. **Click** on **OK**. The Patterns dialog box will disappear. The March columns will show the pattern you selected.

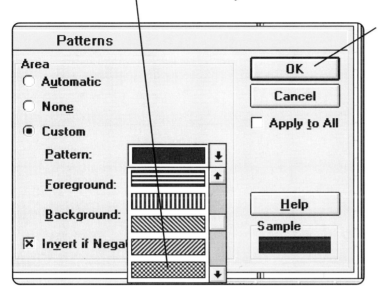

10. **Repeat steps 2 to 8** above for the January and February columns. Now is a good time to play around with various patterns.

Notice the different look!

Notice that the legend has changed to reflect the new patterns.

If you don't like the patterns you chose, you will restore the original patterns in the next section.

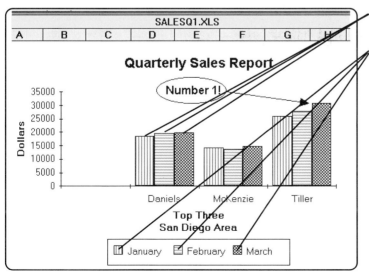

RESTORING THE ORIGINAL PATTERNS

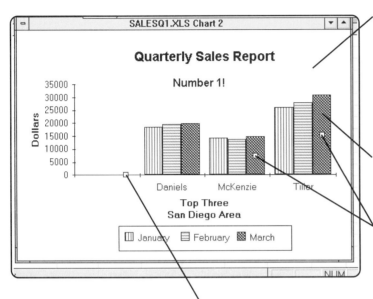

1. **Click twice anywhere** on the **chart**. The SALESQ1.XLS Chart 2 window will appear. If the Chart 2 window is already there, go on to the next step.

2. **Click twice** on **Tiller's March column**. The Patterns dialog box will appear.

Notice that white handles appear on the March columns of two of the three salespeople.

Notice a third white handle appears on the X axis line.

Notice the current custom pattern is shown in the Pattern list box.

3. **Click** on **Automatic** to place a black dot in the circle. The Pattern list box will revert to the original color pattern.

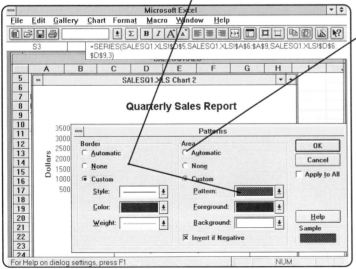

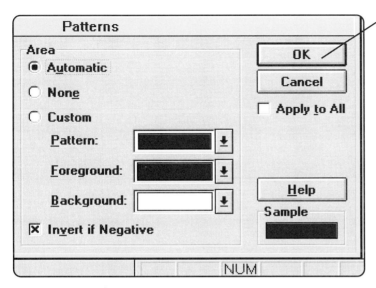

4. **Click** on **OK**. The Patterns dialog box will disappear. The March columns will return to the original pattern.

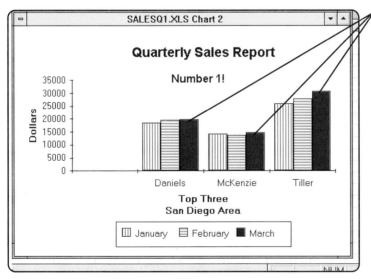

Notice the March columns are restored to the original pattern.

5. **Repeat steps 2 to 5** for the January and February columns. Your columns will be restored to the way they looked at the beginning of this chapter.

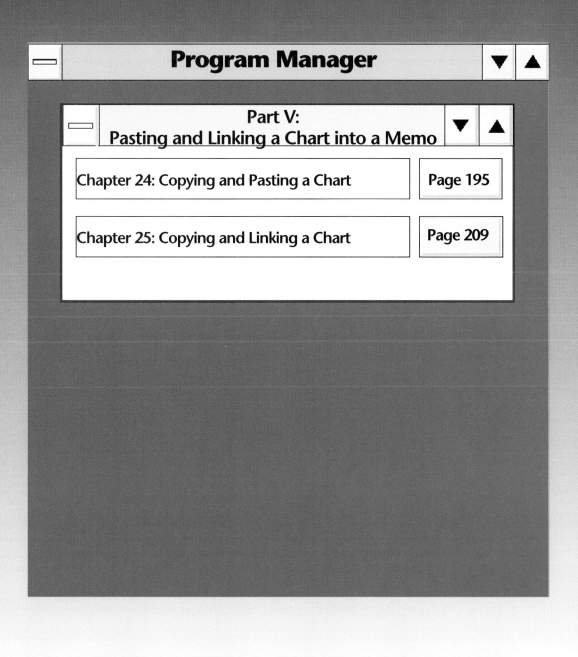

Program Manager

Part V:
Pasting and Linking a Chart into a Memo

Copying and Pasting a Chart

One of the great features of Windows is that you can copy text, clip art, worksheets, charts, graphs, and other objects from one document and paste them into another document. In this chapter you will:

❖ Copy SALESQ1.XLS Chart 2 to the Windows Clipboard

❖ Open a Windows Write document file

❖ Paste SALESQ1.XLS Chart 2 into a Write document and then resize and center the chart

THE COPY AND PASTE PROCESS

The *copy and paste process* consists of three stages:

Stage 1: Copying the Excel chart to the Windows Clipboard

Stage 2: Opening a Windows Write document where you will paste a copy of the chart

Stage 3: Pasting a copy of the chart from the Windows Clipboard into the Windows Write document

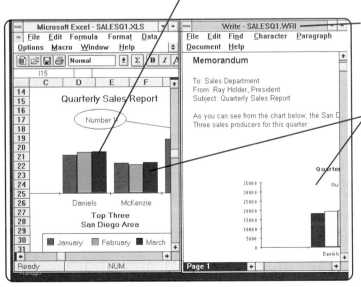

Copying a Chart to the Windows Clipboard

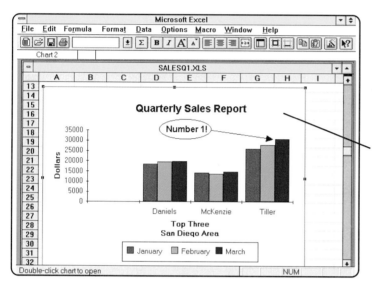

1. **Open** the **SALESQ1.XLS worksheet** containing Chart 2 that you created in Part IV. Refer to Chapter 7, "Opening a Saved File," if you need help.

2. If the chart window is not already active, **click twice anywhere** on the **chart**. The chart will become an active window with a title bar.

3. **Click** on **Chart** in the menu bar. A pull-down menu will appear.

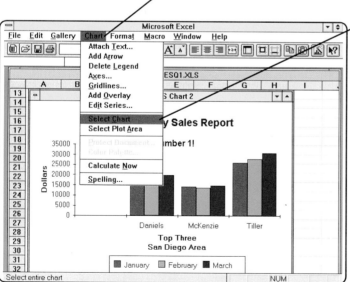

4. **Click** on **Select Chart**. Eight white, square handles will appear inside the border of the chart.

5. **Click** on **Edit** in the menu bar.

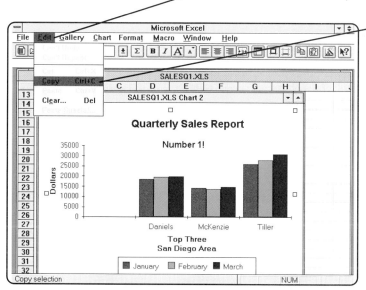

6. **Click** on **Copy**. The chart will be surrounded by a moving border. This border is sometimes affectionately referred to as "running ants."

A copy of the chart is now in the Windows Clipboard and is ready to be pasted into a Windows Write document.

Closing Excel

You do not need to keep Excel running to continue the pasting process. You can close Excel in steps 1 and 2 below. If you want to keep Excel running in the background, do steps 1, 3, and 4 below.

1. **Press and hold** the **Ctrl** key and **press** the **Esc** key (Ctrl + Esc). The Task List dialog box will appear. Microsoft Excel will be highlighted in the Task List.

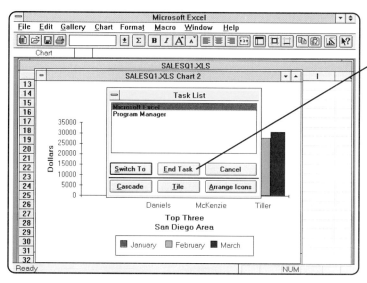

2. **Click** on **End Task**. The Program Manager window will appear.

3. **Click** on **Program Manager** to highlight it.

4. **Click** on **Switch To**. The Program Manager window will appear. Excel will remain in the background if you did not close it.

Opening a Windows Write Document

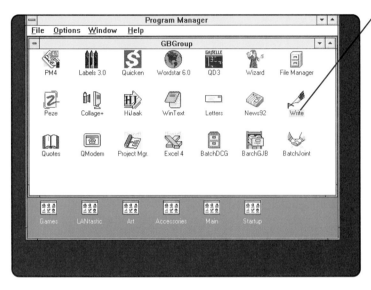

1. **Click twice** on the **Windows Write icon**. (On your computer the Write icon may be in the Windows Accessories group.) The Windows Write window will appear. The title bar will read "Write - (Untitled)." Your Write window may appear in a different place or be a different size than the one shown in this example.

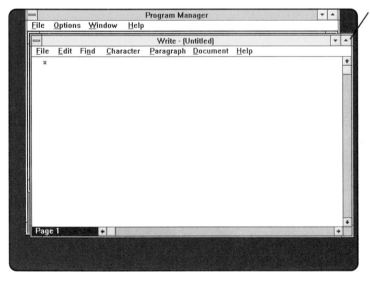

2. **Click** on the **Maximize button (▲)** on the right of the Write menu bar. The Windows Write window will fill the screen.

In the example beginning on the next page, we have prepared a sample word processed memo in Windows Write. You do not need to prepare this memo to paste the SALESQ1.XLS Chart 2 into the Write document.

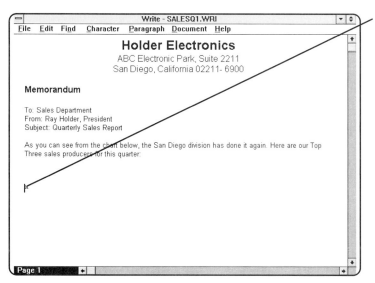

3. Press Enter as many times as needed to **move the cursor** to the spot on the document where you want to paste the copy of Chart 2.

Pasting the Chart

1. Click on **Edit** in the menu bar. A pull-down menu will appear.

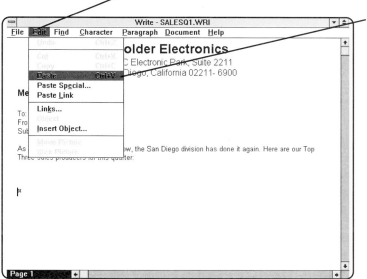

2. Click on **Paste**. Chart 2 will appear in the document.

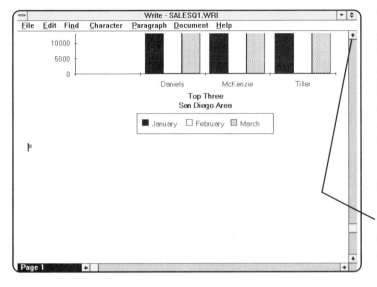

The copy and paste process from Excel to Windows Write mysteriously gives you a view of the bottom of the chart in black and white. If you have a color printer installed in Windows, then the chart will be in color on your screen.

3. **Click repeatedly** on ⬆ on the scroll bar to bring the chart into full view.

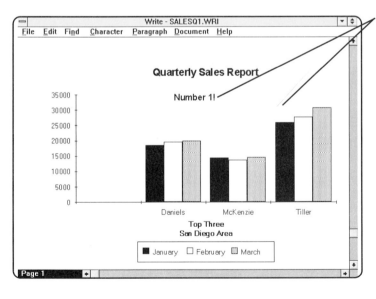

Notice that both the ellipse and the arrow you created in Chapter 21 were not copied to this document. Excel only copies items that are embedded in the chart. And for some reason, arrows and ellipses were not programmed in Excel as embedded items.

SIZING AND CENTERING THE CHART

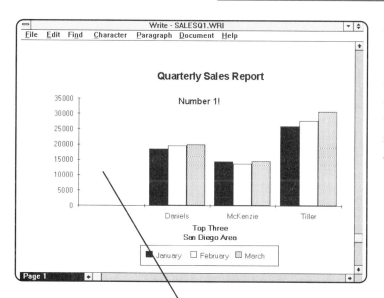

Notice that the chart is quite large. Follow the steps below to reduce its size. Once it is reduced, the chart will be off center in the document. Follow the steps in the next section to center the chart.

Sizing the Chart

1. **Click anywhere** on the **chart**. It will become highlighted in black.

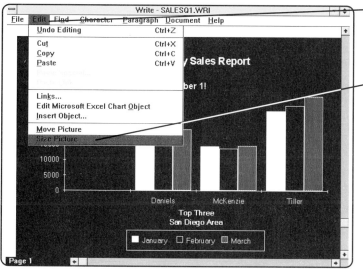

2. **Click** on **Edit** in the menu bar. A pull-down menu will appear.

3. **Click** on **Size Picture**. The pull-down menu will disappear. The black highlighting will disappear and the chart will be surrounded by a faint, gray border.

The pointer will turn into a box shape (⬚).

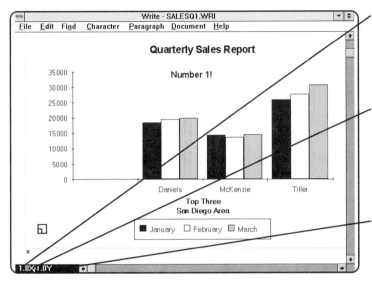

Notice that a sizing scale appears at the bottom of your screen to the left of the scroll bar.

The numbers and letters, **1.0X/1.0Y**, tell you that the chart's X axis width is at 100% (1.0) and the chart's Y axis height is at 100% (1.0).

The numbers in this box will change as you resize the chart.

4. **Move** the **box-shaped pointer** to the **bottom-left corner** of the gray **border**. The goal is to reduce the chart to 70% of its original size. You will know you have reached this goal when the numbers in the sizing box read **.7X/.7Y**.

5. When the pointer "catches" the **corner of the border, move** the **mouse** and **drag** the **border up** and **to the right** to reduce the width and height of the chart.

Caution: *Do not press the mouse button* until you have finished your sizing operation. If you do, you may suddenly find yourself with a black highlighted chart. In that case, repeat steps 2, 3, and 4 to begin sizing again.

6. Click on the **left mouse button** when the sizing box reads **.7X/.7Y**. The chart will be highlighted in black and will appear in its new, reduced size.

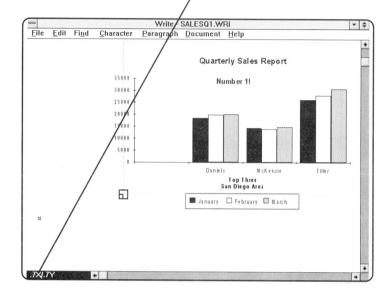

Notice that the resized chart is off center. In the next section you will center the chart on the page.

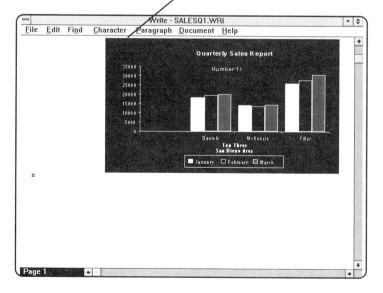

Centering the Chart

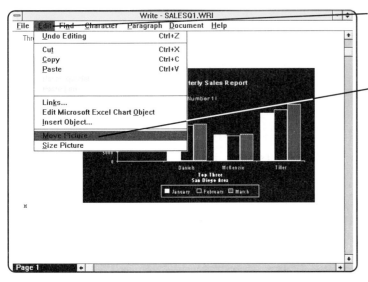

1. **Click** on **Edit** in the menu bar. A pull-down menu will appear.

2. **Click** on **Move Picture**. The black highlighting will disappear and the chart will be surrounded by a faint border. The same pointer that you used in sizing the chart will appear in the center of the chart.

3. **Move** the **pointer** to the **left** until the border of the chart is **centered** across the page. Notice that you can only move the border of the chart to the left or to the right. The chart itself will not move until you click the mouse button.

Caution: *Do not click the mouse button* until the chart is repositioned.

4. **Click** on the **left mouse button** when you have reached the approximate position you want. The chart will appear where you positioned the border and will be highlighted in black.

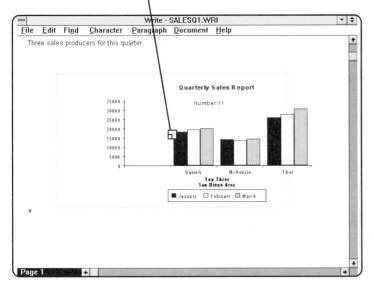

5. Click anywhere on the **document**. The black highlighting will disappear.

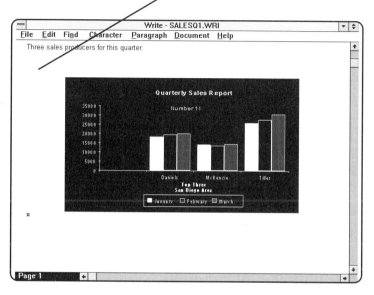

Here is the finished product: A Windows Write memorandum containing a resized copy of the SALESQ1.XLS Chart 2!

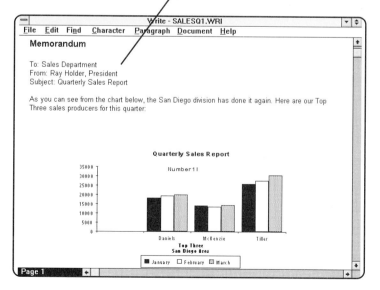

If you use a different Windows-based word processing program, the process of copying and pasting will be similar.

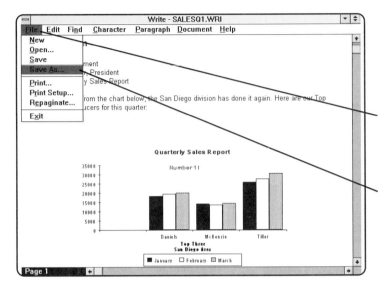

SAVING THE WRITE DOCUMENT

1. **Click** on **File** in the menu bar. A pull-down menu will appear.

2. **Click** on **Save As**. The pull-down menu will disappear. The Save As dialog box will appear.

If you have previously saved this document (as we have in this example) the File Name text box will contain the highlighted filename. If you have not previously saved this document, the File Name text box will be empty and the cursor will be flashing in it, ready for you to enter a name.

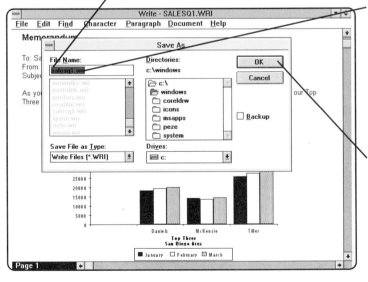

3. **Type salesq1** if salesq1.wri is not already in the box. Excel will automatically add the .WRI extension to the filename. If it is already there, skip this step.

4. **Click** on **OK**. The Save As dialog box will disappear and the Write SALESQ1.WRI document window will appear. Your file is saved!

CLOSING THE WRITE DOCUMENT

1. **Click** on **File** in the menu bar. A pull-down menu will appear.

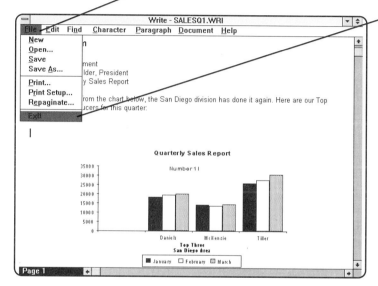

2. **Click** on **Exit**. The pull-down menu and the Write SALESQ1.WRI document window will disappear. The Program Manager window will appear.

A chart like the one you pasted in this chapter will not be updated automatically when you make a change in the original Excel chart. This paste method is useful if you want a document in which the chart does not change every time you change the data in your worksheet. For example, if you want to create a memo with a chart of last month's sales figures, you would not want the chart to reflect this month's updates to the worksheet.

In the next chapter, you will *paste and link* the SALESQ1.XLS Chart 2 to a Windows Write document. Any change made in an Excel chart that has been paste-linked to a Write document will be automatically reflected in the Write version of the chart.

Copying and Linking a Chart

Another terrific feature of Windows is that you can *link* a worksheet chart into a word processed document. When a worksheet chart is linked to a word processed document, *any changes made in the worksheet chart are automatically reflected* in the document. In this chapter you will:

❖ Copy SALESQ1.XLS Chart 2 to the Windows Clipboard

❖ Open a Windows Write document file

❖ Paste-link the SALESQ1.XLS Chart 2 to a Windows Write document

❖ Observe the link in action

THE COPY AND LINK PROCESS

The copy and link process described in this chapter consists of four stages:

Stage 1: Copying the Excel chart to the Windows Clipboard

Stage 2: Keeping Excel running in the background

Stage 3: Opening a Windows Write document into which you will paste-link the chart

Stage 4: Paste-linking a copy of the Excel chart from the Clipboard into the Windows Write document

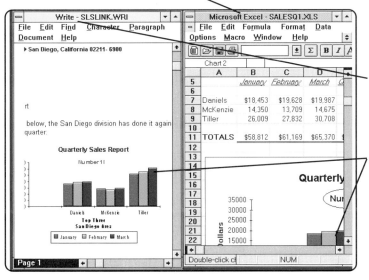

Copying a Chart to the Windows Clipboard

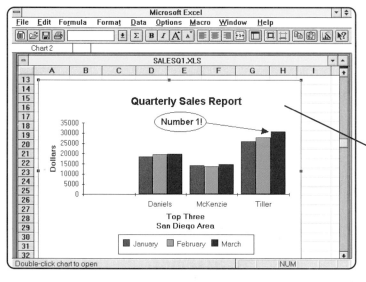

1. **Open** the **SALESQ1.XLS worksheet** containing Chart 2 that you created in Part IV. Refer to Chapter 7, "Opening a Saved File," if you need help.

2. **Click twice anywhere** on the **chart** if the chart window is not active.

Chart 2 will become an active window with a title bar.

Do not be surprised if you experience déjà vu in the first part of this chapter. The process of pasting and linking a chart to a Write document is similar to simply pasting a chart, but the results are very different! Also, please note that if you are using a version of Windows that is older than version 3.1, you will not be able to link an Excel chart to the Write document.

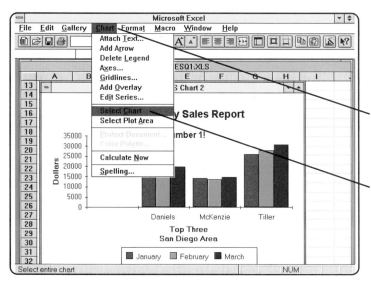

3. **Click** on **Chart** in the menu bar. A pull-down menu will appear.

4. **Click** on **Select Chart**. You will see eight white handles on the inside of the border of the chart, as shown in the example at the top of the next page.

5. **Click** on **Edit** in the menu bar. A pull-down menu will appear.

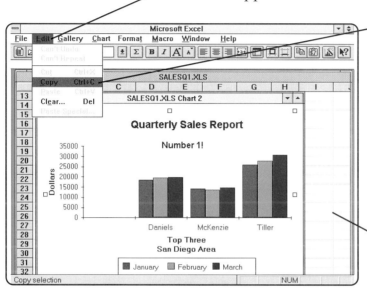

6. **Click** on **Copy**. The pull-down menu will disappear. The chart will be surrounded by a moving border as shown in the example below. A copy of the chart is now in the Windows Clipboard and is ready to be linked into a Windows Write document.

7. **Click once anywhere** off the **chart** to remove the title bar.

Running Excel in the Background

In order to link Chart 2 to a Windows Write document, Excel must be running in the background.

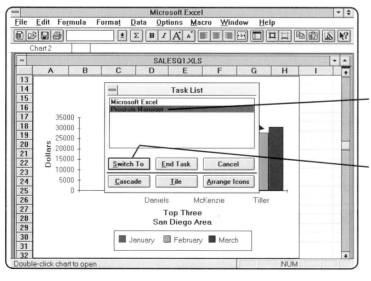

1. **Press and hold** the **Ctrl** key and **press** the **Esc** key (Ctrl + Esc). The Task List dialog box will appear.

2. **Click** on **Program Manager**. It will become highlighted.

3. **Click** on **Switch To**. The Program Manager window will appear in the foreground. The Excel window will move to the background.

Opening a Windows Write Document

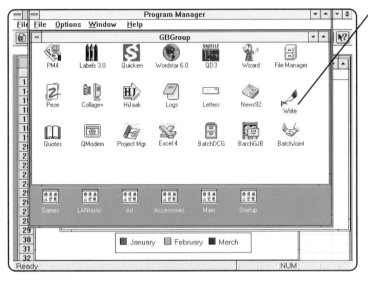

1. **Click twice** on the **Windows Write icon**. (On your computer the Write icon may be in the Windows Accessories group.) The Windows Write window will appear. The title bar will read "Write - (Untitled)." Your Write window may appear in a different place or be a different size than the one shown in this example.

Caution: Do not use the Write document you created in Chapter 24 unless you first delete the chart you have already pasted in it. Otherwise, you will end up with two copies of the same chart in one Write document. It can be very confusing!

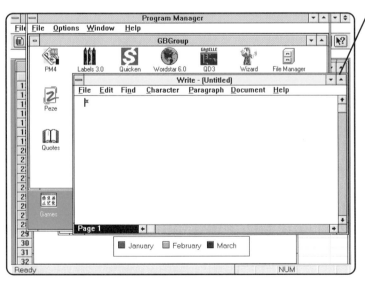

2. **Click** on the **Maximize button** (▲) on the right side of the Write - (Untitled) menu bar. The Windows Write window will fill the screen.

In the example beginning on the next page, we have prepared a sample word processed memo in Windows Write. You do not need to prepare this memo to paste-link the SALESQ1.XLS Chart 2 to the Write document.

Linking the Chart

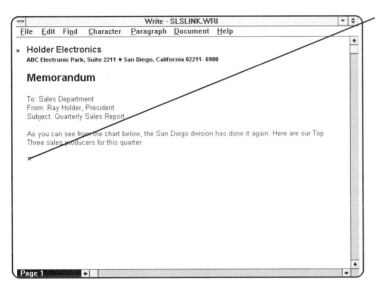

1. **Press Enter** as many times as needed to **move the cursor** to the spot on the document where you want to paste-link the copy of Chart 2. Remember, a copy of Chart 2 is currently in the Windows Clipboard.

2. **Click** on **Edit** in the menu bar. A pull-down menu will appear.

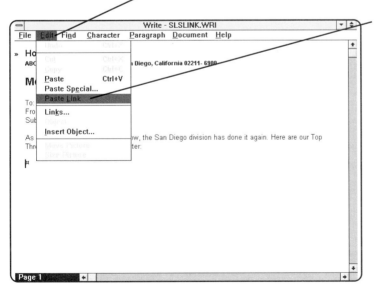

3. **Click** on **Paste Link**. Chart 2 will appear in the document.

Chart 2 may be placed in an unexpected position like the screen in the next example. The copy and paste-link process from Excel to Windows Write initially gives you a view of the bottom of the chart.

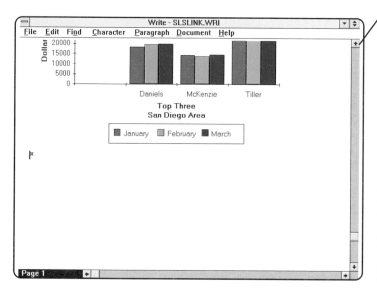

4. Click repeatedly on the ↑ on the scroll bar to bring the chart into view.

Color! Good News – Bad News

Unlike the copy and paste process you did in Chapter 24, the copy and paste-link process results in a linked chart initially displayed in color. That's the good news. The bad news is that after you close and reopen the Write document file, the chart will be displayed in black and white. For those folks with a color printer, the news is still good. If you have a color printer, the chart will remain in color on your screen.

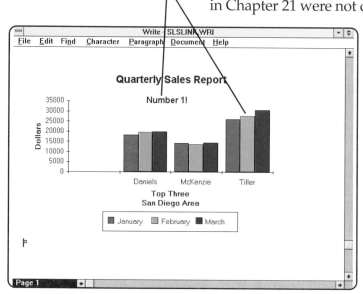

Notice that both the ellipse and the arrow you created in Chapter 21 were not copied to this document. Excel was not programmed to link the arrow and the ellipsis to other documents.

Sizing and Centering the Chart

1. Size and center the **chart** so that it looks like the example on the next page. If you need help sizing and centering the chart, see the section "Sizing and Centering the Chart" in Chapter 24.

VIEWING EXCEL AND WINDOWS WRITE SIDE BY SIDE

To really appreciate how a link works, you must see it in action. In this section you will place the Excel worksheet and the Windows Write memo side by side (called *tiling*). Next, you will enlarge each program window so that you can see more of each window. Finally, you will change a number on the Excel worksheet and see the change reflected in the Write memo.

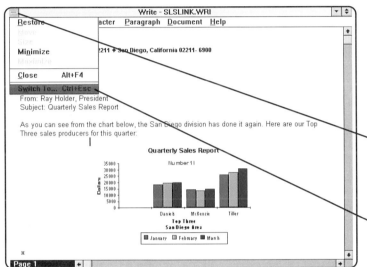

1. **Click** on the **Control menu box** (⊟) on the left of the title bar. A pull-down menu will appear.

2. **Click** on **Switch To**. The Task List dialog box will appear.

Caution: To place two programs side by side (tile), no other programs can be running except Program Manager, which must be minimized. If your Task List shows programs other than the three listed in the example here, close them before proceeding.

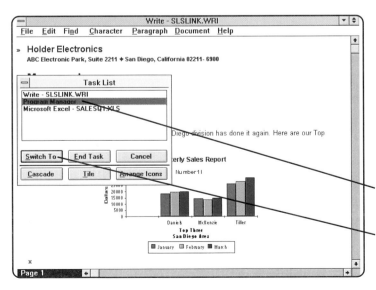

3. **Click** on **Program Manager**.

4. **Click** on **Switch To**. The Program Manager window will appear.

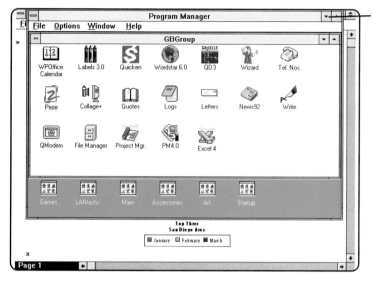

5. **Click** on the **Minimize button** (▼) on the right of the Program Manager title bar. The Program Manager screen will disappear. The Write document window will move to the foreground.

6. **Click** on the **Control menu box** (⊟) on the left of the Write title bar. A pull-down menu will appear.

7. **Click** on **Switch To**. The Task List dialog box will appear.

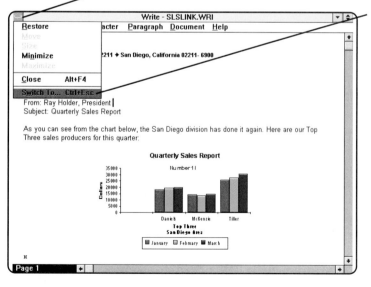

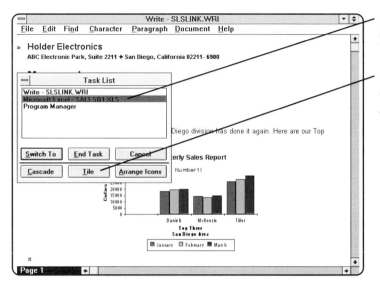

8. **Click** on **Microsoft Excel**.

9. **Click** on **Tile**. The two windows, Write and Excel, will appear side by side.

Enlarging the Two Windows

To get a better view, you must enlarge the two windows.

1. **Place** the **pointer** on the **bottom edge** of the **Write window**. The pointer will turn into a two-headed arrow.

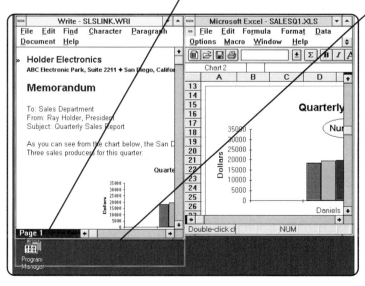

2. **Press and hold** the mouse button as you **drag** the **edge** of the window to the **bottom** of the screen. As you drag, the border of the window will expand. It's okay to cover the Program Manager icon.

3. **Release** the mouse button. The Write window will expand to the bottom of the screen.

4 **Repeat steps 1 to 3** to **enlarge** the **Excel window**.

5. Click repeatedly on the **scroll bar arrows** on *both windows* until your view approximates the one in this example. (If the scroll bars are missing in one of the windows, see below.) You want to be able to see the chart columns on the Write window and, at the same time, see the worksheet sales figures on the Excel window. You may have to fiddle with the two scroll bars in each window to get there.

If there are no scroll bars on the Excel window and it looks like this example, it means that the worksheet window has not been maximized.

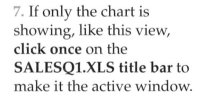

6. Click twice on the **SALESQ1.XLS title bar**. The view will change to the one in the example above and scroll bars will appear. Didn't work? Check your current view.

7. If only the chart is showing, like this view, **click once** on the **SALESQ1.XLS title bar** to make it the active window.

8. Now **click twice** on the **title bar**.

If you find tiling a frustrating experience, join the club. Eventually, most people get the hang of it.

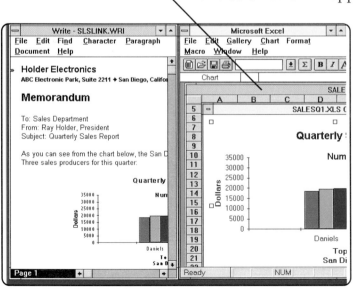

TESTING THE LINK

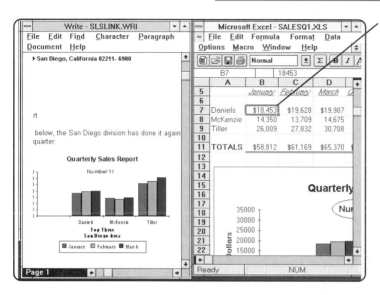

1. **Click** on **B7** on the worksheet. The cell will be surrounded by a black border. The current sales numbers for this cell will appear in the formula bar.

2. **Type 60000**. The number will automatically appear in the formula bar and in the cell as you type.

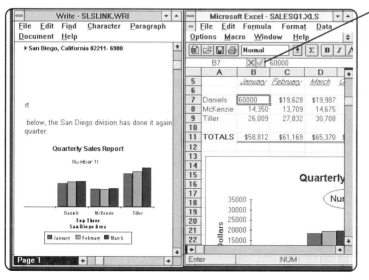

3. **Click** on ✔ and watch the fun. Daniels' January column will automatically enlarge in both windows. The link works!

If you lost the color in the linked chart, see the next page.

OOPS . . . Kiss the Color Good-bye

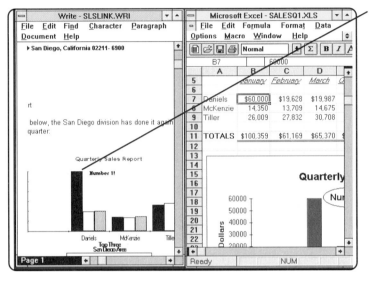

Notice that the chart in the Windows Write column instantly lost its color when you made a change in the worksheet numbers. Your chart is now black and white. If the color in the linked chart in Write disappeared earlier, you probably accidentally clicked on the chart. When you do this, Excel removes the color unless you have a color printer installed.

Just for Fun!

Try changing other numbers on the worksheet and watch the resulting changes in the Write document chart.

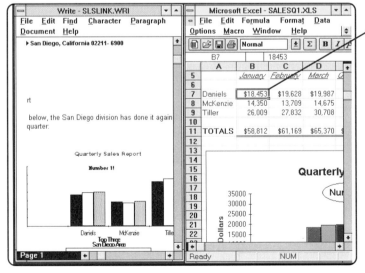

If you are going to use the Excel worksheet to complete other chapters in this book, remember to change the numbers on the worksheet back to their original amounts.

Tip: An easy way to return to the original figures is to exit Excel without saving. See the next section to do that.

EXITING EXCEL

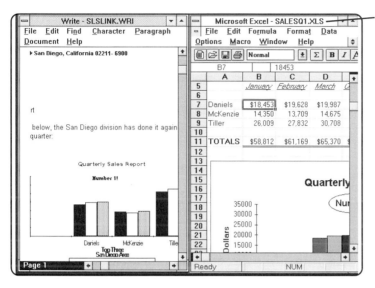

1. **Click** on the **Excel SALESQ1.XLS title bar** to make Excel the active window if it is not already active.

2. **Press and hold** the **Alt** key and **press** the **F4** key (Alt + F4). The Microsoft Excel dialog box will appear.

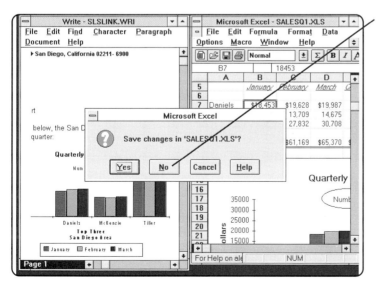

3. **Click** on **No**. The Excel window will close. Any changes you made in the "Just for Fun" section will not be saved.

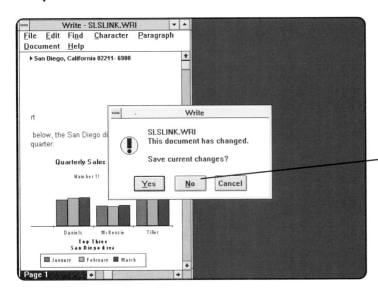

CLOSING WRITE

1. **Press and hold** the **Alt** key and **press** the **F4** key (Alt + F4). The Write dialog box will appear.

2. **Click** on **No**. The Write window will disappear and the Program Manager icon will appear at the bottom of your screen. The changes to the Write document will not be saved. If you want to save them, **click** on **Yes**.

OPENING THE PROGRAM MANAGER WINDOW

1. **Click twice** on the **Program Manager icon**. The Program Manager window will appear.

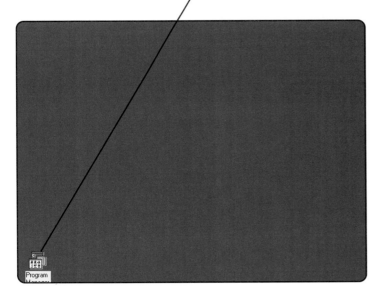

WHAT NEXT?

There are many exciting features of Excel left to explore. We hope this introduction has given you an understanding of its capabilities. We hope, also, that you have gained confidence in your ability to master its complexities.

Experiment! Have fun!

Program Manager

Part VI: Appendix

Appendix: Installing Excel 4	Page 225

Installing Excel 4

In this appendix you will:

❖ Make backup copies of your Microsoft Excel disks
❖ Install Microsoft Excel 4
❖ Move Excel to your customized group window
❖ Print the Excel README text files
❖ Delete the Excel group window
❖ Give the Excel program icon a shorter title

BACK UP YOUR EXCEL 4 DISKS!

Before you start, make certain that you have a supply of formatted disks handy.

1. **Type diskcopy a: a:** (or b: b:, depending on the drive you use) and **press Enter**. There is a space after "diskcopy" and after the first "a:" The message, "Insert SOURCE diskette in drive A: (or B:)" will appear.

```
C:\diskcopy a: a:

Insert SOURCE diskette
in drive A:

Press any key to con-
tinue...

Copying 88 tracks
18 sectors per track,
2 side(s)

Insert TARGET diskette
in drive A:
```

2. **Insert** the **Excel disk** to be copied in **drive A** (or B). Remember, if you are copying *from* a 1.4MB (megabyte) floppy, you must copy *to* a 1.4MB floppy. DOS will not let you use the Diskcopy command to copy to a different capacity floppy.

Note: If you know File Manager or have a better copy program, feel free to use a different method.

3. **Press Enter** and **follow the directions** on your screen. Remember, the *SOURCE* diskette is the Excel 4 disk. The *TARGET* diskette is the blank formatted disk. It takes a number of passes to copy a disk completely. Continue to insert the same SOURCE disk and the same TARGET disk until you are asked if you want to copy another diskette.

```
Insert SOURCE diskette in drive A:

Press any key to continue...

Insert TARGET diskette in drive A:

Press any key to continue...

Insert SOURCE diskette in drive A:

Press any key to continue...

Insert TARGET diskette in drive A:

Press any key to continue...

Volume Serial Number is 22DG-101B

Copy another diskette (Y/N)?
```

4. **Type y** to begin the process again with the second Excel disk and a second blank TARGET disk. Repeat the process until all the disks are copied.

INSTALLING THE PROGRAM

1. **Open Windows** by **typing win** at the DOS prompt (C:\>). The Program Manager opening screen will appear. Your screen may look different from this one.

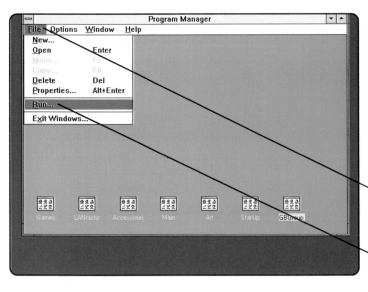

2. **Insert** your **backup** copy of Microsoft Excel **Disk 1-Setup** in drive A. (Be certain to use your backup copies throughout the installation. Put your original disks in a safe place).

3. **Click** on **File** in the menu bar. A pull-down menu will appear.

4. **Click** on **Run**. The Run dialog box will appear.

Notice that the cursor is flashing in the Command Line text box. When you start typing it will disappear.

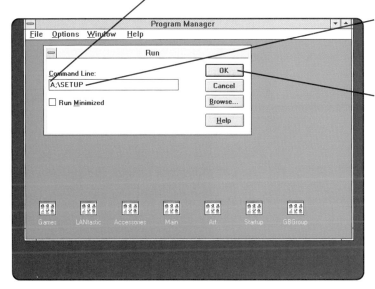

5. **Type A:\SETUP** (or B:\SETUP) in the Command Line text box.

6. **Click** on **OK**. The hourglass will appear briefly along with a Microsoft Setup message box that says "Starting Microsoft Excel Setup..." Next, the User Information for Microsoft Excel dialog box will appear.

Notice that the cursor is flashing in the Name text box. When you start typing it will disappear.

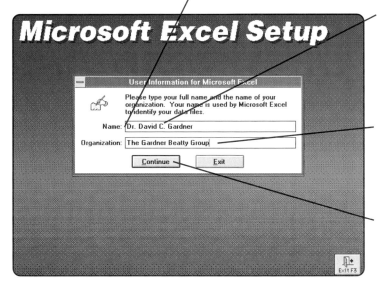

7. **Type** your **full name** in the Name text box and then **press Tab** to move the cursor to the Organization text box.

8. **Type** the **name of your organization**, if applicable, in the Organization text box.

9. **Click** on **Continue**. A second User Information for Microsoft Excel dialog box will appear.

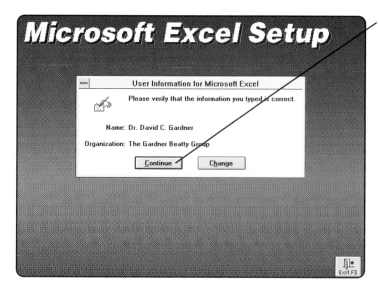

10. Click on **Continue** if the information is correct. The Microsoft Excel 4.0 Setup dialog box will appear.

If the information is not correct, **click** on **Change**. The previous dialog box will reappear. After making your corrections, **click** on **Continue** (see step 9) to return to this dialog box and complete step 10.

11. Click on **Continue**. A smaller Microsoft Excel 4.0 Setup dialog box will appear in the foreground.

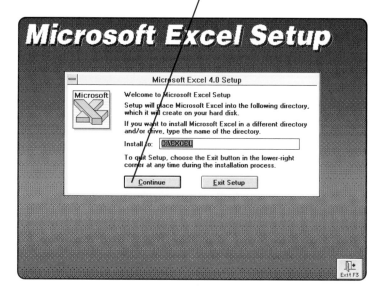

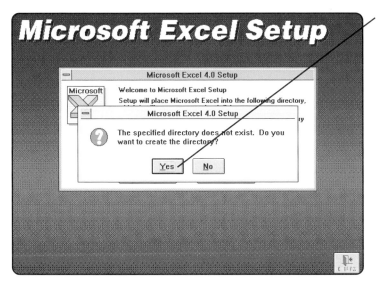

12. **Click** on **Yes**. A message box will appear briefly which says "Please wait while Setup checks for available disk space." Then the Microsoft Excel for Windows 4.0 dialog box will appear.

13. **Click** on **Complete Installation** to follow the procedures in this book.

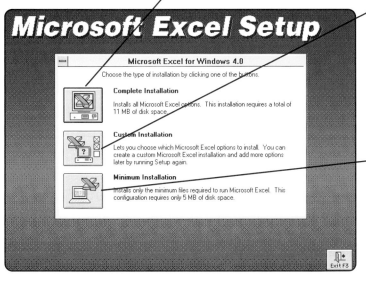

❖ If you are an experienced Excel user you may **click** on the **Custom Installation option**. The Custom Installation procedure will not be illustrated here.

❖ If you are worried about how much disk space you have, **click** on the **Minimum Installation option**. The Minimum Installation procedure will not be illustrated here.

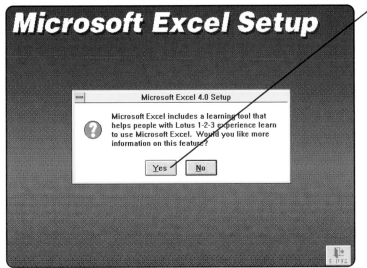

14. **Click** on **Yes** if you have had experience with Lotus 1-2-3. The Enable Help for Lotus 1-2-3 Users dialog box will appear. Otherwise, **click** on **No**.

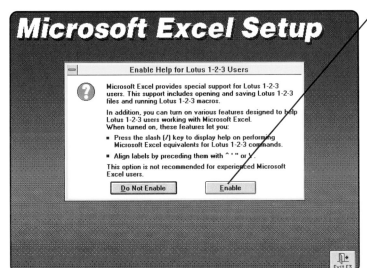

15. **Click** on **Enable** if you want to use the Lotus 1-2-3 options described on the screen. If you are an experienced Excel user (or have never used Lotus 1-2-3), **click** on **Do Not Enable**. The Microsoft Excel 4.0 Setup dialog box will appear.

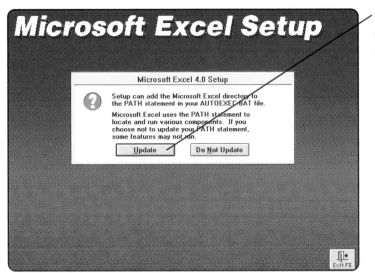

16. **Click** on **Update**. Excel will begin copying files from Disk 1.

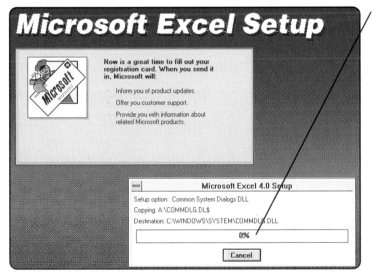

Notice that Excel will show you the percentage of files copied as it copies them from the disk in drive A. This may take a while, so be patient. (The first time we installed Excel 4 we thought something was wrong because nothing seemed to be happening for quite some time. Then all of a sudden Excel began to whiz through the copying!)

When the files on Disk 1 have been copied, an additional Microsoft Excel 4.0 Setup dialog box will appear in the center of your screen. If you have a screen saver, it may blank your screen. If this happens, press any key to return to the installation screen.

17. **Remove Disk 1** from drive A and **insert Disk 2** in drive A.

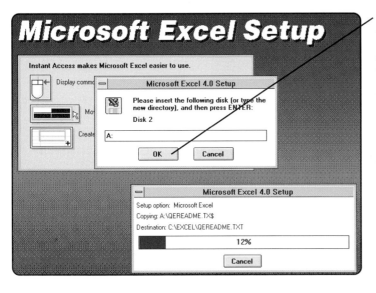

18. **Click** on **OK** or **press Enter**. The second Setup dialog box will disappear. Excel will begin copying the files on Disk 2.

If copying seems to take forever, just hang in there. You are doing fine!

19. **Remove Disk 2** from drive A and **insert Disk 3** in drive A.

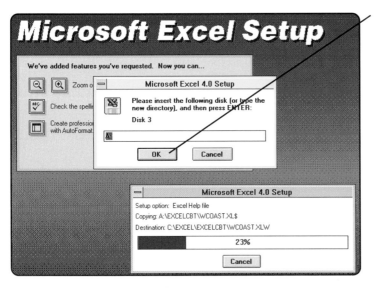

20. **Click** on **OK**. Excel will begin copying the files on Disk 3. **Repeat this process** for Disk 4 and Disk 5.

When Excel has completed copying all the files in Disk 5, the following message will appear briefly on the screen: "Please wait while Setup updates WIN.INI and other settings."

This also may take a while. Just hang in there!

Then the Microsoft Excel Setup is complete! dialog box will appear.

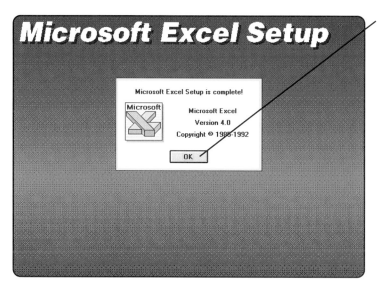

21. **Click** on **OK**. The Microsoft Excel 4.0 group window will appear. It may appear in a different size or location than the one shown here.

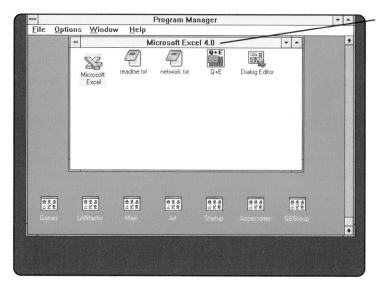

Congratulations! You have successfully installed Excel.

You can leave the Excel program icons in this group window or move them to another group window. Many people have a group window in which they store the programs they use the most. If you want to do that, go on to the next page to move the Excel program icons to your own customized group window. If not, you can go to the Introduction at the beginning of this book, select your first learning goal, and begin using Excel 4.

MOVING AND SETTING UP EXCEL IN YOUR CUSTOMIZED GROUP WINDOW

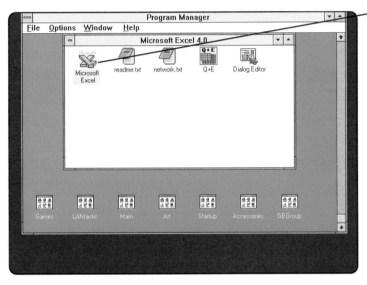

1. **Move** the mouse pointer to the **Excel program icon**.

2. **Press and hold** the mouse button as you **drag** the **Excel program icon** to your personal work group icon at the bottom of your Program Manager screen. The icon will change briefly to a circle and then change back to the Excel program icon. Your screen and group icons may be different from these.

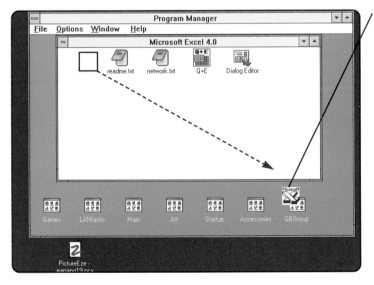

3. **Release** the mouse button when the Excel icon is on top of your personal work group icon. The Excel icon will disappear into your personal work group icon. In this example, the Excel icon is now located in the GBGroup group icon.

4. **Repeat the process** for the Dialog Editor icon and the Q+E icon. Do not move the readme.txt icon or the network.txt icon. In the next section, you will print the information contained in the .TXT files.

Printing Excel Information Text Files

Software companies constantly update their products. This means that some of the newest information is not in the printed documentation, but is contained in text files that are installed with your software. It's a good idea to print these files so that you will have a paper copy for reference.

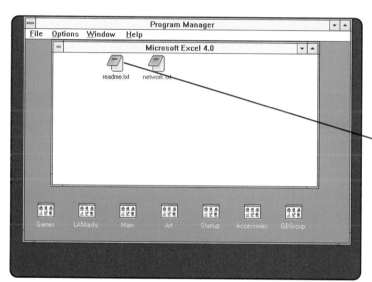

1. **Click twice** on the **readme.txt icon**. The Notepad – README.TXT document window will appear.

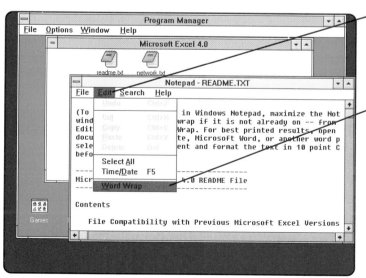

2. **Click** on **Edit** in the Notepad – README.TXT menu bar. A pull-down menu will appear.

3. **Click** on **Word Wrap**. The pull-down menu will disappear. The README.TXT document file is now ready to print.

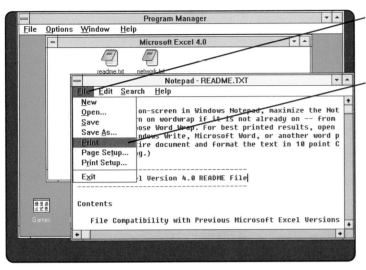

4. **Click** on **File** in the menu bar. A pull-down menu will appear.

5. **Click** on **Print**. The Notepad, Now Printing, README.TXT message box will appear. The Print Manager icon will appear at the bottom of the screen.

When the document begins to print, the message box will disappear. When printing is complete, the Print Manager icon will disappear.

Closing the Notepad – README.TXT Document Window

1. **Click** on **File** in the menu bar. A pull-down menu will appear.

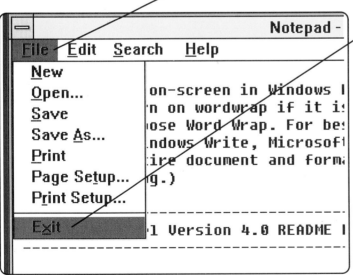

2. **Click** on **Exit**. The pull-down menu and the Notepad – README.TXT window will disappear.

3. To print and then close the NETWORK.TXT file, **repeat steps 1 to 5** in the previous section, "Printing Excel Information Text Files," and steps 1 and 2 above.

Deleting the Excel Group Icon

You have moved the Excel program icons to your work group window and have printed the text files. Now you can delete the Excel group icon since it no longer serves a useful purpose.

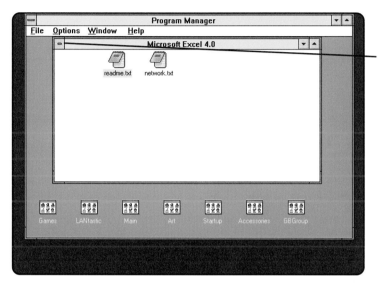

1. **Click twice** on the **Control menu box** (⊟) on the left of the Excel group window title bar. The Excel group window will disappear and the Excel group icon will appear at the bottom of your Program Manager screen.

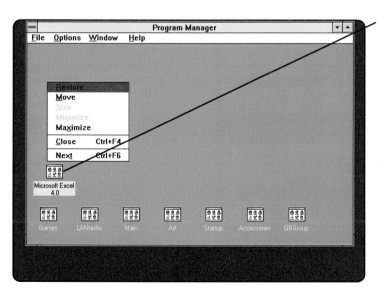

2. **Click once** on the **Excel group icon**. (Make certain that you do not click twice.) The Excel group icon title will become highlighted and a pop-up menu will appear. Ignore the pop-up menu and go on to step 3.

3. **Click** on **File** in the Program Manager menu bar. A pull-down menu will appear and the pop-up menu will disappear.

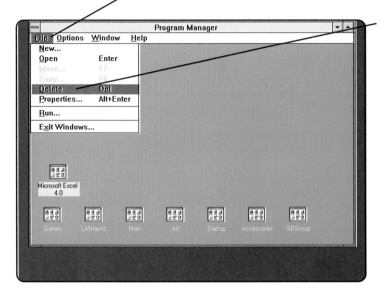

4. **Click** on **Delete**. The pull-down menu will disappear. The Delete dialog box will appear.

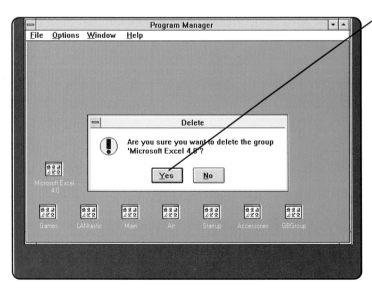

5. **Click** on **Yes**. The Delete dialog box will disappear, the Excel group icon will be deleted, and you will be returned to Program Manager.

Renaming the Excel Program Icon

If you would prefer a shorter title for the Excel program icon, you can shorten it or change it completely by following the steps below. In this example, you will change the title of the icon to Excel 4.

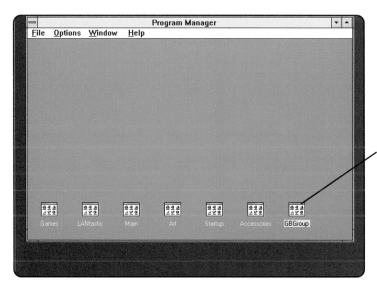

1. **Click twice** on the **group icon** that contains your Excel program. The group window will open. In this example, the Excel icon is in the GBGroup group window.

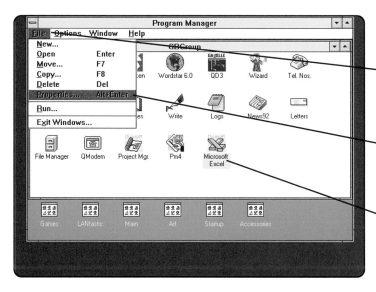

2. **Click once** on the **Excel program icon** to highlight it.

3. **Click** on **File** in the menu bar. A pull-down menu will appear.

4. **Click** on **Properties**. The Program Item Properties dialog box will appear.

Notice the highlighted two-line title. This must be highlighted to change the title of the icon.

Notice that the name "Microsoft Excel" in the Description text box is highlighted. This means that the cursor is set so you can type in the Description text box.

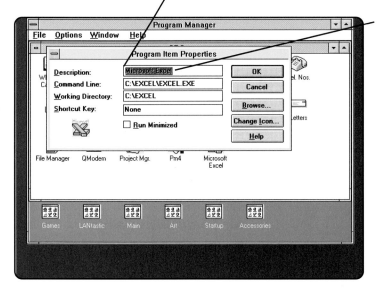

5. **Type Excel 4**. The highlighted "Microsoft Excel" text will disappear from the Description text box. It will be replaced by "Excel 4."

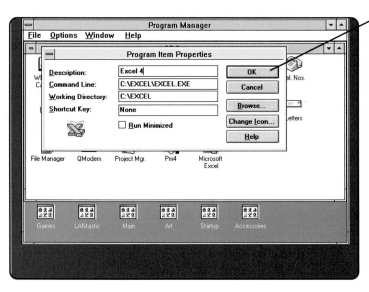

6. **Click** on **OK**. The Program Item Properties dialog box will disappear. The title, "Excel 4," will appear underneath the Excel program icon.

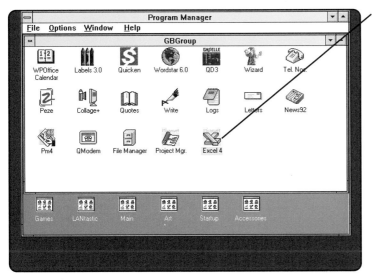

Notice the one-line title for the Excel program icon.

Now that you have successfully installed Excel 4 and organized your personal work area, you are ready to return to the Introduction at the beginning of this book, select your first learning goal, and begin learning about and using Excel 4.

Index

If You Like This Book... You'll Love The Newsletter!

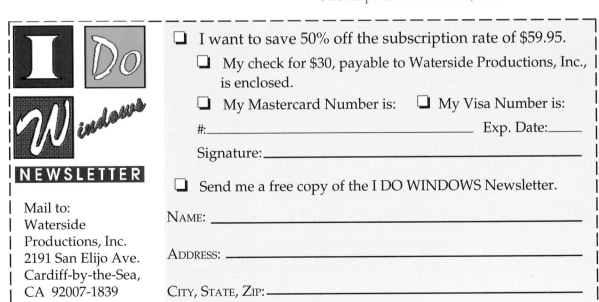